The Amazing Adventures of
MR. GRANT MONEY

STRIVE press

Dear Reader,

Thank you for embarking on this exciting journey with "The Amazing Adventures of Mr. Grant Money." I'm thrilled to share with you the valuable insights and lessons contained within these pages, lessons that have empowered countless individuals and organizations to achieve remarkable success in their grant acquisition endeavors.

Grant funding is a powerful tool, and this book is designed to be your companion as you navigate the intricate world of grant writing. Within these stories lie not just narratives but essential lessons that will guide you toward securing funding for your projects. As you read and engage with the exercises, I hope you find inspiration and actionable strategies to elevate your grant acquisition efforts to new heights.

Throughout my career, I've had the privilege of assisting many individuals starting from ground zero, witnessing their transformation into successful grant seekers. The stories and lessons in this book encapsulate some of the crucial insights that have contributed to their achievements.

However, I must take a moment to introduce you to another invaluable resource—the "Grant Writing That Gets Funded" training. This training has been a cornerstone in the success stories of numerous students and organizations. Tailored for beginners and intermediate grant professionals, it offers clear and comprehensive guidance. Participants not only absorb my exclusive Grant Writing Success Formula but also leave with a personalized 30-Day Grant Empowerment Strategy and Grant Readiness Resource.

Our training has played a pivotal role in agencies securing substantial funding, ranging from $25,000 to millions, in a remarkably short period. You can witness some of these success stories at WowTheyDidIt.com. I am confident that with our support, you could be the next success story, unlocking a bountiful windfall of grant funding for your endeavors.

Imagine the impact on your team as they gain insights, adopt best practices, and leverage industry secrets, giving your agency a competitive edge. This training could be the pivotal factor that distinguishes you from others, ensuring you secure the grants you pursue.

As Kjeld Linstead, a past participant, expressed, "Thanks again for the grants class a few months ago... Since taking your class, I have landed nearly $4 Million in state and federal grants for the City of Redlands."

For more information about the Grant Writing That Gets Funded training, please visit GrantWritingClasses.org. You can also secure your spot by calling 1-888-293-0284. This investment in your organization's financial stability is a strategic move towards a more prosperous future.

Best Regards,

Rodney

Grant Central USA

P.S. Be sure to try our free grant training at StrategicGrantWriting.com.

The Amazing Adventures of
MR. GRANT MONEY

Harvesting Hope:
The Global Odyssey
of Mr. Grant Money

VOLUME ONE

RODNEY WALKER

STRIVE press

Chief Editor: Laine Minerales
Editorial Assistant: Daniel Tuano
Production Supervisor: Joerje Galo
Electronic Composition: Jairus Agoncillo
Photographer: Studio 5404
Executive Marketing Manager: Jimmy Moore

Discover the breadth of our series, encompassing a myriad of crucial topics. Delve into the realms of grant acquisition, college scholarships, entrepreneurship, social impact, philanthropy, and beyond. Unearth a treasure trove of knowledge and empowerment within our diverse collection. Explore the wealth of insights awaiting you across these transformative series.

To inquire about utilizing The Amazing Adventures of Mr. Grant Money books in the classroom, securing licensing, and exploring special pricing for bulk orders, kindly contact us at info@grantcentralusa.com.

ISBN: 978-0-9659275-0-5

Printed in the United States

Dedication

In loving memory of my dear mother, Shirley Walker,
Your boundless encouragement, kindness, and nurturing spirit have
profoundly influenced the person I became. This book is dedicated to you,
in remembrance of the countless sacrifices you made for my well-being.
Your love continues to be the enduring foundation of my life.

With heartfelt love and eternal gratitude,
Rodney

PREFACE

The Adventures of Mr. Grant Money: A Journey of Transformation

In the world of grant acquisition, where dreams take flight on the wings of well-crafted proposals, where passion meets purpose, and where communities are transformed through the power of giving, I invite you to embark on a remarkable journey. These adventures are not just a recounting of tales but a testament to the evolution of a grant professional who started with the humblest of beginnings and emerged as a Master Grant Acquisition Specialist.

Over two decades in the making, these stories are a blend of my real-life experiences as a grant professional. They unfold the lessons learned, the challenges faced, and the victories achieved. From the time when I was a novice, wide-eyed and eager to write my first grant proposal, seeking a mere $25,000 for a youth development program, to the present, where I've had the privilege of assisting thousands of individuals and organizations worldwide each year, this journey is one of profound transformation.

It all began with the idea of sharing inspiring tales through a series of blog posts, offering snippets of wisdom and knowledge to those in the world of grants. Yet, as I put pen to paper, these stories took on a life of their own, weaving together to form something magical, something special. What started as a caterpillar of inspiration morphed into a butterfly waiting for you to leap onto its wings and embark on a series of captivating journeys.

This collection is intended to educate and entertain, to offer fresh ideas and insights for seasoned veterans of the grant profession, to guide and inspire newcomers, and perhaps even awaken the curiosity of a young student unaware of the incredible world of grant acquisition.

In this adventure, we'll dive into the core of grant writing, explore the depths of fundraising, and unearth the hidden treasures of effective philanthropy. We'll laugh, we'll learn, and we'll leap beyond the boundaries of the ordinary.

But at the heart of it all, this is a testament to the power of belief. For, as you'll discover, belief is the force that propels dreams into reality. As you journey through these tales, remember one word: BELIEVE!

Now, dear reader, join me as we venture forth into the world of Mr. Grant Money's adventures. Let's explore, learn, and transform together. The journey begins with a single page, and the possibilities are endless.

TABLE OF CONTENT

Introduction

Granting Miracles: The Windy City's Savior of Hope for Hearts   9

Riverside's Grant Alchemist: The Magical Transformation of a City   14

Grant Dreams: The Power of Partnership in New York City   20

Sunrise of Success: Mr. Grant Money's Arizona Triumph   27

Style and Substance: Mr. Grant Money's Graceful Journey   33

Swaying to Success: Mr. Grant Money's Miami Rendezvous   39

From Novice to Maestro: Mr. Grant Money's Reflective Journey   45

The Seven Pillars of Grant Acquisition: Mr. Grant Money's Parisian Revelation   51

Unlocking Grants: Marilyn's Journey with Mr. Grant Money's Guide   57

From Caribbean Waves to Grant Wins: Mr. Grant Money's Journey   64

Afterward   70

About the Author   71

Boost Your Grant Game: Additional Resources   72

INTRODUCTION

Welcome to The Amazing Adventures of Mr. Grant Money, Volume 1, where you'll embark on a thrilling journey into the captivating world of grants, philanthropy, and the extraordinary life of the enigmatic Mr. Grant Money. Within these pages, you'll discover ten riveting stories that encapsulate the heart and soul of grant acquisition.

1. Granting Miracles: The Windy City's Savior of Hope for Hearts unveils the transformative power of grants in the Windy City.

2. Riverside's Grant Alchemist: The Magical Transformation of a City delves into the enchanting story of how grants can change the course of an entire city.

3. Grant Dreams: The Power of Partnership in New York City brings you the tale of collaborative efforts to manifest grant dreams in the Big Apple.

4. Sunrise of Success: Mr. Grant Money's Arizona Triumph reveals the art of achieving triumph and success in the land of the rising sun.

5. Style and Substance: Mr. Grant Money's Graceful Journey provides insight into the graceful and elegant journey that is the hallmark of Mr. Grant Money.

6. Swaying to Success: Mr. Grant Money's Miami Rendezvous takes you to the enchanting city of Miami, where success and grants dance in unison.

7. From Novice to Maestro: Mr. Grant Money's Reflective Journey illustrates how one can evolve from a novice to a master in the realm of grant acquisition.

8. The Seven Pillars of Grant Acquisition: Mr. Grant Money's Parisian Revelation unfolds the seven key pillars of successful grant acquisition.

9. Unlocking Grants: Marilyn's Journey with Mr. Grant Money's Guide details the transformative journey of a grant seeker with Mr. Grant Money as their guide.

10. From Caribbean Waves to Grant Wins: Mr. Grant Money's Journey takes you on a voyage through the Caribbean, where the allure of grants meets the serenity of island life.

This book is a gem for grant writing instructors, college and university students learning about grants, new grant writers, seasoned grant professionals, fundraisers, grant consultants, nonprofit organizations, executive directors, government agencies, and faith-based organizations alike. Mr. Grant Money's captivating narratives and expert guidance will inspire, educate, and empower you.

What this book isn't is a dry, technical manual on grant writing. It's an exciting adventure where the wisdom of Mr. Grant Money serves as your compass. Each story is followed by exercises to help you implement similar strategies, discussion questions to deepen your understanding, powerful quotes to keep you inspired, and one BIG Idea you can incorporate into your own grant acquisition practices. There are even interesting word search puzzles awaiting you.

So buckle up for a thrilling journey, as we explore the world of grants, one captivating adventure at a time. Get ready to unlock your full grant acquisition potential, because the adventure begins now.

GRANTING MIRACLES

THE WINDY CITY'S SAVIOR OF HOPE FOR HEARTS

The Extraordinary Tale of Mr. Grant Money and the Nonprofit Miracle in the Windy City

Once upon a time in the bustling city of Chicago, there lived a man named Grant Money, but everyone knew him as Mr. Grant Money. He wasn't your average Chicagoan; he possessed a unique talent that made him legendary in the city's nonprofit circles. With his unrivaled charisma, smarts, and enviable expertise, he had the power to turn struggling organizations into Grant Heroes.

One sunny morning, the struggling nonprofit organization known as "Hope for Hearts" found itself at its wits' end. Their mission to provide healthcare and support to underserved communities was admirable, but their coffers were empty, and their hopes were dwindling. It was then that they heard whispers of Mr. Grant Money, a man with a legendary reputation for securing grants that could turn even the direst of situations around.

Hope for Hearts decided to take a leap of faith and invited Mr. Grant Money to their small office tucked away in the heart of Chicago's South Side. As soon as he walked in, Hope for Hearts knew they were in for a treat. Dressed in a dapper suit and wearing a charming smile, Mr. Grant Money exuded an aura of confidence and expertise.

"Good day, ladies and gentlemen of Hope for Hearts," he greeted them with a flourish. "I've heard your tale of woe, and I'm here to make your dreams come true."

Over the following weeks, Mr. Grant Money worked his magic. He started by meticulously researching potential grant opportunities from small foundations and government agencies. Armed with a list of prospects, he began to craft compelling grant proposals that would tug at the heartstrings of even the most stoic reviewers.

But it wasn't just his grant writing skills that set Mr. Grant Money apart. He was a master networker and knew precisely how to make influential connections. He hosted charity galas, organized community events, and worked his charm to secure meetings with key decision-makers in the funding world.

Slowly but surely, Hope for Hearts began to see results. They received their first small grant, which Mr. Grant Money had secured from a local foundation.

The organization was elated, but Mr. Grant Money knew they could do even better.

He continued to work his magic, securing larger grants from state agencies and national foundations. He coached the staff on effective grant management and reporting, ensuring they exceeded expectations at every turn.

One day, Hope for Hearts received a phone call that left them in disbelief. It was from a prestigious national foundation, offering them a grant that exceeded their wildest dreams. They were now able to expand their services to more communities, hire more staff, and truly make a difference on a grand scale.

Hope for Hearts had gone from struggling to thriving, all thanks to the amazing adventures of Mr. Grant Money. He had not only secured the funding they needed but had also transformed them into Grant Heroes, exceeding their expectations beyond their wildest dreams.

As for Mr. Grant Money, he tipped his hat and disappeared into the Chicago skyline, ready to embark on his next adventure, leaving Hope for Hearts with a legacy of success and a city full of nonprofits eager to seek his magical touch. And so, the legend of Mr. Grant Money continued to grow, one grant at a time, in the Windy City and beyond.

"Grant Money isn't just a name; it's a promise. I'm on a mission to turn nonprofits into heroes and ensure that no dream goes unfunded. The power of a grant can make miracles happen."

Exercise: "Crafting Effective Grant Proposals"

Based on the story of Mr. Grant Money's success in securing grants for the nonprofit organization "Hope for Hearts," here's an actionable exercise to help someone improve their grant proposal writing skills:

Objective: Learn how to craft compelling grant proposals that resonate with potential funders and secure financial support for your nonprofit or project.

Instructions:

1. Research: Select a nonprofit organization or project you're passionate about or involved in. Research potential grant opportunities that align with the mission and goals of the organization. Identify at least three grant opportunities to target.

2. Analyze Successful Proposals: Study examples of successful grant proposals online, if available, or through your network. Pay attention to the structure, language, and storytelling elements that make these proposals compelling.

3. Storytelling Practice: Write a draft grant proposal for one of the selected grant opportunities. In your proposal, incorporate storytelling techniques, just as Mr. Grant Money did in the story. Share a compelling narrative about the organization's mission and the impact the grant will have on its beneficiaries.

4. Peer Review: Share your draft with a peer, mentor, or colleague for feedback. Ask them to evaluate the clarity, emotional appeal, and alignment with the grant's requirements.

5. Revise and Finalize: Based on the feedback received, revise your proposal. Make sure it's concise, clear, and aligns with the grant guidelines. Focus on making an emotional connection with potential funders.

6. Submission: Submit your final grant proposal to the selected funding opportunities. Keep track of submission deadlines and requirements.

7. Evaluation: After submission, monitor responses and follow up as needed. This exercise not only improves your grant writing skills but also offers valuable real-world experience.

"In the world of grants, I'm not just a Grant Master Acquisition Specialist; I'm a dream weaver. I turn nonprofits into Grant Heroes, one proposal at a time, and watch them soar."
- Mr. Grant Money

Discussion Questions

1. What qualities and skills made Mr. Grant Money so effective in helping struggling nonprofit organizations like Hope for Hearts? How did his charisma, expertise, and networking abilities play a role in their transformation?

2. The story highlights the power of grant funding in enabling nonprofits to make a significant impact. What are some of the challenges and opportunities nonprofit organizations face when seeking grants, and how does Mr. Grant Money address these challenges?

3. Mr. Grant Money not only secured funding but also transformed Hope for Hearts into a successful organization. What are the key elements of his approach that led to Hope for Hearts' transformation? How did he go beyond securing grants to make them "Grant Heroes"?

4. The story portrays Hope for Hearts as a symbol of struggling nonprofits in Chicago. How does the story reflect the broader challenges faced by nonprofit organizations, especially those serving underserved communities in urban areas?

5. The story leaves us with the idea of Mr. Grant Money's ongoing adventures in helping nonprofits. What lessons can other nonprofit organizations and grant-seekers learn from his success in the Windy City and beyond?

Big Idea "PhilanthroLink: Bridging Dreams and Donors for a Better Windy City"

The story of Mr. Grant Money illustrates the transformative impact of connecting resources to organizations with a noble cause. "Miracle Matchmaker" could be a digital platform or organization that aims to match philanthropic donors with struggling nonprofit organizations in the Windy City. This platform would serve as a bridge between donors who are willing to provide grants and nonprofits seeking funding.

The concept could include a sophisticated algorithm that matches donors with organizations based on their mission, needs, and values. It would not only help nonprofits like Hope for Hearts find the support they need but also ensure that donors can see their contributions making a tangible impact on the underserved communities. This idea would take inspiration from the remarkable work of Mr. Grant Money and create a sustainable solution to connect funding opportunities with organizations striving to make a difference.

🔍 Word Search

Enter the enchanting world of Mr. Grant Money and the extraordinary nonprofit miracle in the Windy City with this word search puzzle. Journey through the heart of Chicago and the legendary tale of 'Granting Miracles: The Windy City's Savior of Hope for Hearts.'

In this puzzle, discover the words related to the extraordinary adventures of Mr. Grant Money. Can you find all the hidden words that capture the essence of this remarkable story?

Now, here are the 15 words for the word search puzzle based on the story:

E	P	H	C	G	I	H	P	N	K	H	M	C	G
K	X	I	T	N	E	P	O	H	A	R	A	R	N
R	O	P	N	M	I	R	A	C	L	E	M	C	E
O	E	E	A	E	N	R	O	M	W	A	S	G	R
W	A	A	R	N	O	E	C	E	A	L	I	C	A
T	S	G	G	D	S	R	T	N	R	R	R	H	C
E	C	N	X	U	O	I	O	I	G	R	A	I	H
N	R	H	S	E	M	H	O	G	N	P	H	C	T
Y	E	N	O	M	F	A	P	N	I	P	C	A	L
T	I	F	O	R	P	N	O	N	D	A	A	G	A
S	P	R	O	P	O	S	A	L	N	A	N	O	E
I	E	S	C	E	R	R	N	C	U	P	L	F	H
E	S	I	T	R	E	P	X	E	F	C	F	A	U
I	L	P	C	T	S	U	C	C	E	S	S	R	G

NETWORK
EXPANSION
NONPROFIT
SUCCESS
FUNDING
CHARISMA
GRANT
MIRACLE
HOPE
GALA
PROPOSAL
EXPERTISE
MONEY
HEALTHCARE
CHICAGO

"In the heart of Chicago, a legend was born, not in riches, but in the art of turning hopes into realities. Mr. Grant Money wasn't just a man; he was a beacon of light for nonprofits, an inspiration for all."

RIVERSIDE'S GRANT ALCHEMIST

Riverside's Grant Alchemist: The Magical Transformation of a City

How Mr. Grant Money and His Power House Team Turned $32 Million Dreams into Reality

After Mr. Grant Money's triumphant stint in Chicago, he embarked on a whirlwind tour of cities across the United States, empowering nonprofits and government agencies to secure the funding they needed. His reputation preceded him, and organizations from New York to Los Angeles clamored for his expertise, charm, and savvy style of attracting money.

One fateful day, he arrived in the vibrant city of Riverside, where Mayor Margaret Collins was facing a massive challenge. For three long years, her administration had been desperately trying to secure a coveted federal grant worth a staggering $32 million to revitalize the city's aging infrastructure. Despite their best efforts, they found themselves in a never-ending cycle of rejection letters and missed opportunities.

Mayor Collins had heard of Mr. Grant Money's legendary prowess and knew that she needed to enlist his help. She reached out to him personally and invited him to Riverside to work his magic.

Mr. Grant Money arrived in Riverside with his trademark style and confidence, ready to take on the challenge. He gathered a team of experts, each with their own unique set of skills, under his capable direction. This Power House Team was a force to be reckoned with, and they got to work immediately.

They began by conducting a thorough analysis of the previous grant applications and identified the weaknesses that had led to rejection. Mr. Grant Money's keen intelligence and strategic thinking quickly became evident as he devised a new approach.

First, they revamped the proposal, injecting it with a fresh perspective and a compelling narrative that would capture the hearts and minds of the federal grant reviewers. Mr. Grant Money's charm and charisma came into play as he established connections with key decision-makers in Washington, D.C., making sure Riverside was no longer just another name on a piece of paper.

But Mr. Grant Money had a few tricks up his sleeve, secrets of the trade he had honed over years of grant acquisition. These tricks involved some creative financial wizardry, innovative project planning, and leveraging unconventional resources. They were so effective that they unearthed an additional $7 million in potential funding that no one had even thought possible.

As the submission deadline approached, the entire team worked tirelessly under Mr. Grant Money's guidance, ensuring every detail was perfect. The proposal was a masterpiece, combining heartwarming stories of Riverside's residents with solid data and a strategic vision for the future.

The day of reckoning arrived when the grant award announcements were due. Riverside's hopes were higher than ever, but this time, they were tempered with a sense of confidence, thanks to Mr. Grant Money's expertise.

When the news finally came in, it was a moment of sheer jubilation. Riverside had been awarded the $32 million federal grant they had sought for years. Mayor Collins and her team couldn't believe their eyes as they celebrated their success. And the additional $7 million? Well, let's just say that was a well-guarded secret, known only to Mr. Grant Money and his team.

As he bid farewell to Riverside, Mr. Grant Money left behind a city transformed. Riverside's infrastructure revitalization was now possible, and its future was brighter than ever before.

In the end, the people of Riverside learned a valuable lesson: if you ever have the opportunity to become a client of Mr. Grant Money, you should jump at the chance. In fact, you might want to sign up for his waiting list right away. Because when it comes to securing grants and unlocking hidden funding, there's no one quite like Mr. Grant Money, the man with the magic touch and the power to turn dreams into reality.

Exercise: "The Grant Application Makeover Challenge"

Based on the inspiring story of Mr. Grant Money's transformation of Riverside's grant application, here's an actionable exercise to improve your grant writing skills:

Objective: Practice revamping a grant application to make it more compelling, strategic, and competitive, just like Mr. Grant Money and his Power House Team did for Riverside.

Instructions:

1. Select a Grant Opportunity
- Choose a real or fictional grant opportunity that aligns with the mission of a nonprofit organization or project you care about. Make sure to obtain the grant's guidelines, requirements, and evaluation criteria.

2. Analyze and Identify Weaknesses
- Review the organization's previous grant applications, if available, or create a fictional one. Identify weaknesses, such as lack of clarity, missing components, or insufficient storytelling.

3. Revamp the Proposal
- Rewrite the grant application, incorporating improvements based on the weaknesses you've identified. Focus on the following key areas:

- Narrative: Craft a compelling narrative that highlights the organization's mission, impact, and the problem it aims to solve.

- Data and Research: Include data and research to support the organization's goals and demonstrate the need for the project.

- Strategic Vision: Describe a clear and strategic vision for the project's success, including measurable outcomes and timelines.

- Budget and Financial Planning: Revise the budget section to ensure it is realistic, transparent, and aligned with the project's goals.

- Community Stories: Share personal stories and testimonials from those who have benefited from the organization's work.

4. Creative Financial Strategies:

- Just as Mr. Grant Money used innovative financial strategies, consider how you can improve the financial section of your proposal. Think about potential sources of funding or cost-saving measures that could enhance the project's financial sustainability.

5. Get Feedback:

- Share your revamped grant application with a peer, mentor, or colleague. Ask for feedback on its clarity, persuasiveness, and alignment with the grant guidelines.

6. Finalize and Submit:

- Make the necessary revisions based on the feedback you receive. Ensure your proposal complies with the grant's requirements, and submit it before the deadline.

7. Reflect:

- After submission, reflect on the changes you made and the lessons you learned. Consider how your revamped proposal is more competitive and compelling compared to the original.

This exercise will not only enhance your grant writing skills but also help you better understand the elements that make a grant application stand out and increase its chances of success, just as Mr. Grant Money and his team did for Riverside.

"In the world of grants, it's not just about asking for money; it's about crafting a symphony of purpose and potential. I don't just secure grants; I compose stories that move the world to invest in dreams."
-Mr. Grant Money

Discussion Questions

1. How do you think Mr. Grant Money's approach and strategies differed from the previous attempts made by Mayor Margaret Collins and her team in securing the federal grant for Riverside's infrastructure revitalization?

2. In the story, Mr. Grant Money utilized creative financial wizardry, innovative project planning, and unconventional resources to uncover an additional $7 million in potential funding. What are some ethical considerations that might arise when employing such tactics in grant acquisition, and how can these be balanced with the desire to secure much-needed funding for community projects?

3. The narrative emphasizes the importance of storytelling in the grant proposal, combining heartwarming stories of Riverside's residents with solid data and a strategic vision for the future. How do you think the integration of narrative elements contributes to the success of a grant proposal?

4. Mr. Grant Money's reputation preceded him, and organizations across the United States sought his expertise. Discuss the role of personal branding and reputation in the field of grant acquisition and public service. How can individuals like Mr. Grant Money use their reputation to make a positive impact?

5. The story highlights the transformative impact of securing the federal grant on Riverside's future. In your opinion, how might the successful revitalization of a city's infrastructure positively influence its community, economy, and overall well-being? Additionally, what potential challenges?

💡 Big Idea "The Grant Catalyst Initiative"

Inspired by the remarkable story of Mr. Grant Money and his team, the city of Riverside could establish the "Grant Catalyst Initiative." This initiative would aim to identify and nurture local individuals who possess extraordinary grant acquisition skills, just like Mr. Grant Money. The city would provide training programs, mentorship, and resources to develop these Grant Catalysts who can then work with local nonprofits, government agencies, and community projects to secure the funding they need. By creating a network of local experts, the city can continue to transform and revitalize its infrastructure and community development in a sustainable and ongoing manner. This initiative would also serve as an example for other cities looking to tap into local talent for grant acquisition.

🔍 Word Search

Join us in celebrating the incredible journey of Mr. Grant Money and his Power House Team as they worked their magic in Riverside, turning $32 million dreams into reality. In this word search puzzle, discover the words related to their remarkable story of grant acquisition and the transformation of a city. Can you find all the hidden words that capture the enchanting tale of Riverside's Grant Alchemist?

In this puzzle, discover the words related to the extraordinary adventures of Mr. Grant Money. Can you find all the hidden words that capture the essence of this remarkable story?

Now, here are the 14 words for the word search puzzle based on the story:

V	R	L	M	F	C	R	T	S	H	Y	T	O	T
R	N	O	I	T	A	L	I	B	U	J	R	M	R
S	P	I	O	U	O	N	O	V	F	G	A	A	F
O	L	S	N	M	N	G	C	H	I	R	N	Y	U
A	S	O	C	H	A	R	M	R	L	I	S	O	N
E	P	R	O	P	O	S	A	L	F	V	F	R	D
X	T	L	A	N	R	A	E	A	E	E	O	T	I
P	P	M	O	N	E	Y	E	U	D	R	R	N	N
E	I	P	M	S	N	R	R	A	E	S	M	A	G
R	U	S	U	C	C	E	S	S	R	I	A	R	T
T	C	R	E	A	T	I	V	E	A	D	T	G	R
I	L	M	O	S	N	T	L	X	L	E	I	Y	C
S	A	A	P	N	R	R	T	R	D	C	O	E	E
E	C	E	L	E	B	R	A	T	I	O	N	E	U

FEDERAL
MAYOR
MONEY
PROPOSAL
FUNDING
TRANSFORMATION
SUCCESS
GRANT
JUBILATION
EXPERTISE
CHARM
CELEBRATION
CREATIVE
RIVERSIDE

"Riverside's transformation wasn't just about dollars and cents; it was a testament to the power of passion, strategy, and the unwavering belief that even the most formidable challenges can be overcome. Mr. Grant Money may have been the magician, but Riverside was the stage for a real-life, awe-inspiring magic show."

Grant Dreams: The Power of Partnership in New York City

How Harmony Heights School District Secured $20 Million with Mr. Grant Money's Guidance

As Mr. Grant Money continued his remarkable journey, word of his success stories spread far and wide. Nonprofits and government agencies alike yearned for his guidance, knowing that his unique blend of intelligence, charm, and grant acquisition savvy was worth its weight in gold.

One day, an organization known as "Hopeful Horizons," located in the heart of bustling New York City, caught wind of Mr. Grant Money's legendary reputation. Their financial situation was dire, and they were willing to pay his hefty $100,000 fee to secure his services. They believed they could simply buy their way into his expertise. However, Mr. Grant Money was no ordinary consultant. He was discerning and particular about who he worked with, just as he was with his choice of fine suits and hats.

After careful consideration, he declined their offer, explaining that his clients were carefully chosen and had to be willing to follow his guidance and expertise, not the other way around. He believed in a partnership built on trust, respect, and a shared commitment to the mission.

Unfazed by the rejection, Hopeful Horizons turned to other avenues for help, but their fortunes remained unchanged. It was around this time that a struggling school district in upstate New York, known as "Harmony Heights School District," reached out to Mr. Grant Money.

Harmony Heights faced the looming threat of budget cuts that could potentially devastate their educational programs and opportunities for students. They had heard about Mr. Grant Money's incredible success stories, and they were desperate for his guidance.

Upon reviewing their situation, Mr. Grant Money saw the potential for real change. He agreed to work with Harmony Heights, and together, they embarked on a journey to secure much-needed funding. Mr. Grant Money began by assembling a team of experts in education and grant acquisition, tailoring his approach to their unique needs.

They crafted a power grant acquisition plan that left no stone unturned. It involved identifying underutilized resources, engaging the community in the school's mission, and developing innovative educational programs that aligned with the priorities of grant-giving organizations.

For two consecutive years, Harmony Heights School District followed Mr. Grant Money's guidance diligently. The results were nothing short of spectacular.

They secured a staggering $10 million in grant funding each year, ensuring the continuation of vital educational programs and providing opportunities for countless students.

The success of Harmony Heights left other school districts in New York green with envy. They wondered how this district had achieved such remarkable results while they struggled with budget constraints. Little did they know that not everyone could have a skillful, savvy, and intelligent Master Grant Acquisition Specialist like Mr. Grant Money as their secret sauce.

Mr. Grant Money's success in Harmony Heights had a ripple effect that extended beyond the school district itself. Not only did Harmony Heights thrive academically, but the increased investment in education also revitalized the entire community. Local businesses saw an uptick in customers as the school district's success drew more families to the area. This economic boost not only improved the financial well-being of the town but also fostered a renewed sense of unity and pride among its residents.

Harmony Heights School District became a beacon of hope for other struggling communities, proving that with the right guidance and dedication, they too could turn the tides of financial adversity. It inspired neighboring school districts and nonprofits to reevaluate their approaches to grant acquisition and community engagement. Mr. Grant Money's impact went well beyond the dollars secured; it was a testament to the transformative power of strategic thinking and genuine commitment to a shared mission.

As Mr. Grant Money continued his journey, his story became a symbol of what could be achieved when an individual with expertise, integrity, and a passion for positive change dedicated themselves to a greater cause. His legacy served as a reminder that while grant money was essential, it was the people and their unwavering belief in a common goal that truly made the difference. His adventures were far from over, and as he moved from one city to another, he left a trail of hope, empowerment, and prosperity in his wake, enriching not only the organizations he touched but the countless lives they impacted.

"The true value of my expertise isn't measured in dollars, but in the commitment to a shared mission. You can't buy success; you have to invest in trust, dedication, and the belief that together, we can make dreams come true."
-Mr. Grant Money

Exercise: "The Partnership Challenge"

Based on the story of Mr. Grant Money's emphasis on building a strong partnership with clients, this exercise focuses on developing effective partnerships with nonprofits or organizations to help them secure funding.

Objective: Learn the importance of building strong partnerships and collaboration in the context of grant acquisition and funding opportunities.

Instructions:

1. Select a Nonprofit Partner:
- Identify a nonprofit organization, charity, or community project that you are passionate about or interested in supporting.

2. Research the Organization:
- Conduct thorough research on the selected organization to understand their mission, goals, and current financial situation. Reach out to them to express your interest in collaborating.

3. Initial Meeting:
- Schedule an initial meeting with the organization's leadership or key decision-makers. In this meeting, express your willingness to support their grant acquisition efforts and provide guidance based on your expertise. Emphasize the importance of a partnership built on trust, respect, and a shared commitment to the mission, just as Mr. Grant Money did.

4. Needs Assessment:
- Work closely with the organization to assess their grant acquisition needs and challenges. Identify areas where your skills and expertise can make a significant difference in their grant application process.

5. Strategic Planning:
- Collaboratively develop a strategic grant acquisition plan that outlines key grant opportunities, target donors, and the steps to secure funding. Ensure the plan aligns with the organization's mission and priorities.

6. Engage Experts:
- Like Mr. Grant Money assembled a team of experts, consider bringing in relevant experts in grant writing, project planning, or budgeting to support the organization's grant acquisition efforts.

7. Execute the Plan:
- Implement the grant acquisition plan, working closely with the organization's team. Assist in writing compelling grant proposals, identifying underutilized resources, and engaging the community.

8. Track Progress:
- Regularly monitor the progress of the partnership and grant applications. Keep detailed records of submitted applications, responses, and funding received.

9. Review and Adjust:
- Periodically review the partnership's effectiveness and make necessary adjustments to the grant acquisition plan and approach. Ensure both parties are actively involved and committed to the partnership's success.

10. Celebrate Achievements:
- When successful grants are secured, celebrate the achievements with the organization and its beneficiaries. Recognize the impact of the partnership on their mission and the community.

By engaging in this exercise, you'll experience firsthand the power of building a strong partnership and collaboration with a nonprofit or organization in pursuit of grant funding, just as Mr. Grant Money did with Harmony Heights School District. This exercise not only helps the organization but also provides you with valuable experience in guiding and supporting grant acquisition efforts.

"In the world of grants, my expertise is the golden key that unlocks doors to possibilities. I'm selective, not because I'm exclusive, but because I believe in partnerships fueled by passion, respect, and unwavering dedication."
-Mr. Grant Money

Discussion Questions

1. Mr. Grant Money emphasized the importance of a partnership built on trust, respect, and a shared commitment to the mission when working with organizations. How did this philosophy impact the successful collaboration between Mr. Grant Money and Harmony Heights School District, and what can other organizations learn from this approach?

2. The story mentions that Harmony Heights School District secured $10 million in grant funding for two consecutive years. What specific strategies and tactics did Mr. Grant Money and his team employ to achieve this remarkable result, and how did these strategies differ from those used by other struggling school districts in New York?

3. The story suggests that Mr. Grant Money's involvement with Harmony Heights had a significant impact on the district's educational programs and opportunities for students. Can you provide more details about the specific improvements or initiatives that were made possible by the acquired grant funding, and how they benefited the students and the community?

4. Mr. Grant Money's reputation and expertise are highly sought after. What qualities or characteristics do you think make him a successful grant acquisition specialist, and how do these attributes contribute to his ability to secure substantial funding for the organizations he works with?

5. The story alludes to the envy felt by other school districts in New York when they learned of Harmony Heights' success. What lessons can these other districts draw from Harmony Heights' experience with Mr. Grant Money, and how might they improve their own grant acquisition efforts to secure much-needed funding?

💡 **Big Idea** "The Grant Innovation Fund"

In honor of Mr. Grant Money's innovative approach to securing grants, the city of New York could establish a "Grant Innovation Fund." This fund would support and promote creative and unconventional grant acquisition strategies. Nonprofits and government agencies could apply for grants from this fund to experiment with new, out-of-the-box methods for securing funding.

The most promising and effective strategies could then be scaled up and replicated across the city, benefiting a wide range of organizations. By encouraging innovation in the grant acquisition process, New York City could continue to lead in the field of nonprofit support and grant acquisition, fostering a culture of creative problem-solving and resourcefulness among its organizations.

🔍 Word Search

Join us in uncovering the fascinating journey of Mr. Grant Money, the grant acquisition legend, as he weaves his magic through the world of nonprofits and educational institutions. In this word search puzzle, we've hidden words related to his inspiring story, his approach to partnerships, and his remarkable success.

In this puzzle, discover the words related to the extraordinary adventures of Mr. Grant Money. Can you find all the hidden words that capture the essence of this remarkable story?

Now, here are the 14 words for the word search puzzle based on the story:

N	R	D	M	I	S	S	I	O	N	Y	E	H	S
N	E	M	P	O	W	E	R	M	E	N	T	Y	P
N	O	I	T	A	C	U	D	E	T	M	N	L	E
T	I	I	C	I	R	F	E	A	S	O	P	S	C
E	T	J	E	T	S	T	A	A	M	N	I	M	I
J	O	U	R	N	E	Y	N	R	T	T	L	G	A
E	U	T	M	A	Y	E	A	E	R	M	S	R	L
C	S	F	E	T	N	H	A	E	R	I	A	A	I
H	P	U	T	L	E	S	P	P	S	S	P	N	S
S	N	N	O	U	U	X	I	O	I	H	H	T	T
N	X	D	E	S	E	E	R	V	R	E	A	I	H
S	E	I	T	N	A	S	U	C	C	E	S	S	P
Y	A	N	X	O	H	O	P	E	F	U	L	E	E
D	N	G	A	C	H	I	E	V	E	M	E	N	T

FUNDING
ACHIEVEMENT
SUCCESS
PARTNERSHIP
JOURNEY
GRANT
MISSION
CONSULTANT
HARMONY
SPECIALIST
EXPERTISE
EDUCATION
EMPOWERMENT
HOPEFUL

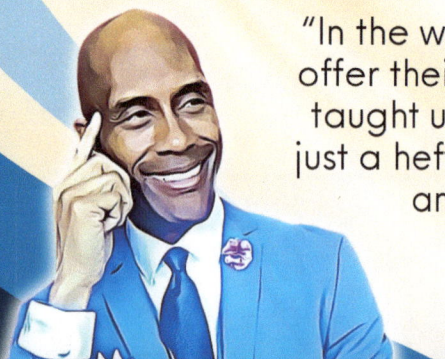

"In the world of grant acquisition, there are many who offer their services, but the legend of Mr. Grant Money taught us that true transformation requires more than just a hefty fee. It's a partnership built on shared values and a commitment to the greater good."

SUNRISE OF SUCCESS

The Amazing Adventures of
MRGRANTMONEY

Sunrise of Success: Mr. Grant Money's Arizona Triumph

How Unity and Strategy Turned a Sunny State into a Grant Oasis

In the world of grant acquisition, there was one name that shone brighter than the rest, and it was none other than Mr. Grant Money. He was a man who played by his own rules, refusing to engage in the cutthroat competition that sometimes plagued the industry. Unlike other consultants who tore down their competition to build themselves up, Mr. Grant Money's style, charm, intelligence, and winning track record spoke for themselves.

One chilly winter morning, as snow blanketed the ground in a very cold and unnamed state, a rival consultant was known for his ruthless tactics. He would stop at nothing to undermine his competition, spreading rumors and sowing discord in the pursuit of personal gain. But not Mr. Grant Money. He had no time for such pettiness. Instead, he focused on helping his clients and letting his results do the talking.

With clients lining up to secure his coveted expertise, Mr. Grant Money decided to turn his attention to the sunny landscapes of Arizona, where two city government departments were in dire need of financial assistance to innovate and better serve their community. The departments had been struggling, and their leaders were at odds, which was impeding progress.

Mr. Grant Money possessed an uncanny intuitive ability to see beyond the surface issues and identify the core problems. He recognized that the real stumbling block for these departments was their leadership. So, before diving into grant applications and fundraising strategies, he set out to mend the rift and create a cohesive team.

With his characteristic charm and diplomacy, Mr. Grant Money orchestrated meetings and team-building activities that brought the department heads together. He helped them recognize the shared goals and aspirations they had for their community. As the tension melted away, a newfound sense of unity and purpose emerged.

Once the leadership issues were resolved, Mr. Grant Money and his team got to work crafting a winning grant acquisition plan. They leveraged their collective intelligence to identify innovative programs and projects that would not only address community needs but also align perfectly with the priorities of grant-giving organizations.

The results were nothing short of spectacular. Thanks to Mr. Grant Money's strategic guidance, the two city government departments secured a massive $4 million grant that would propel their community forward into a brighter future. The community would see improved services, innovative programs, and a better quality of life—all thanks to Mr. Grant Money's remarkable touch.

As the Arizona sun shone down on the city, Mr. Grant Money left behind a legacy of success, unity, and transformation. His adventures continued, his next destination unknown but eagerly anticipated. With clients lining up and a reputation that preceded him, wherever Mr. Grant Money went, one thing was certain: there would be a major windfall of success in his wake. If you ever have the chance to seek out the expertise of this Master Grant Acquisition Specialist, don't hesitate—your community and organization might just be the next to benefit from his extraordinary touch.

> "
>
> In the world of grants, the noise of competition fades into obscurity when you let your results speak. I don't play games; I play to win, and my track record is the finest testament to my success.
> -Mr. Grant Money

Exercise: "The Unity-Building Workshop"

Based on the story of Mr. Grant Money's success in fostering unity among city government departments, this exercise focuses on improving teamwork and unity within an organization, which is essential for a successful grant application process.

Objective: Learn how to build unity and resolve internal conflicts within a team or organization to enhance collaboration in grant acquisition efforts.

1. Select a Team or Organization:
- Choose a team, department, or organization that you are a part of, or one you are interested in supporting for this exercise. This could be a nonprofit, a community group, or any team working on a project or grant application.

2. Identify Areas of Discord:
- Reflect on any internal conflicts, disagreements, or lack of unity within the team or organization that might be hindering progress toward common goals, just as the city government departments faced in the story.

3. Team-Building Activities:
- Organize team-building activities, workshops, or meetings to help address these areas of discord. These activities should focus on improving communication, fostering trust, and promoting a shared vision.

4. Facilitate Discussion:
- If you are a team member, initiate open and honest discussions with your colleagues or team members to identify the underlying causes of discord. Encourage them to share their concerns and feelings in a safe and respectful environment.

5. Set Shared Goals:
- Encourage the team or organization to collectively set shared goals and priorities that align with the mission and grant acquisition objectives. Define a clear, unified purpose that everyone can rally behind.

6. Collaborative Problem-Solving:
- When conflicts or disagreements arise, facilitate collaborative problem-solving sessions. Encourage team members to work together to find solutions and compromises that benefit the team as a whole.

7. Training and Development:
- If necessary, provide training or resources to improve specific skills or competencies within the team that may be contributing to discord. This could include communication, leadership, or conflict resolution training.

8. Regular Check-Ins:
- Implement regular check-in meetings or activities to monitor progress toward unity and shared goals. Encourage open communication and feedback.

9. Celebrate Achievements:
- Celebrate milestones and achievements as a team. Recognize and reward collaborative efforts and the positive impact on the organization's mission and goals.

10. Track Progress:
- Keep records of how the team's unity and collaboration have improved over time. Note any positive changes in team dynamics, communication, and outcomes.

This exercise is not only valuable for grant acquisition but also for overall team or organization success. Fostering unity and resolving internal conflicts can lead to a more cohesive and effective group, as demonstrated by Mr. Grant Money's approach in the story.

> Building bridges is more valuable than burning them. My style isn't about tearing others down; it's about lifting communities up. With charm and strategy, I craft a legacy of transformation and unity.
> -Mr. Grant Money

Discussion Questions

1. The story underscores the importance of unity and leadership within organizations as a precursor to successful grant acquisition. How crucial was Mr. Grant Money's intervention in mending the rift between the department heads in Arizona, and what specific lessons can organizations draw from this experience in improving their internal dynamics?

2. Mr. Grant Money's approach in Arizona involved orchestrating meetings and team-building activities to create a cohesive team. Can you provide examples of the types of activities or strategies he might have used to foster unity among the department heads, and how might these techniques be applied to other organizations facing similar challenges?

3. The story emphasizes that the grant acquisition plan crafted by Mr. Grant Money's team leveraged collective intelligence to identify innovative programs and projects. Can you elaborate on the process of how they identified these innovative initiatives, and how might other organizations replicate this approach to align with the priorities of grant-giving organizations?

4. The results of Mr. Grant Money's work were described as "nothing short of spectacular." Can you provide more details about the specific outcomes and impacts of the $4 million grant on the Arizona community, including how it improved services, innovative programs, and the quality of life for its residents?

5. The story leaves the anticipation of Mr. Grant Money's next destination. What qualities or strategies do you think make him consistently successful in his grant acquisition work, and how can other communities and organizations proactively prepare to benefit from his expertise when he arrives in their area?

💡 **Big Idea** "Grant Harmony Leadership Initiative"

Taking inspiration from Mr. Grant Money's approach to mending conflicts and fostering teamwork, the "Grant Harmony Leadership Initiative" could be established in Arizona. This initiative would focus on offering leadership training and conflict resolution programs specifically tailored to leaders in government departments, nonprofits, and community organizations. The program would aim to not only develop effective leaders but also foster collaboration and unity within teams. By investing in the personal and professional growth of leaders, this initiative would create a more conducive environment for successful grant acquisition and community development. The "Grant Harmony Leadership Initiative" could serve as a model for other states looking to improve leadership and collaboration within their organizations.

🔍 Word Search

Step into the world of grant acquisition with the enigmatic Mr. Grant Money, a man whose reputation outshines the competition. In this word search puzzle, we invite you to discover the hidden words that capture the essence of his remarkable journey, from his refusal to engage in cutthroat competition to his ability to transform communities through strategic grant acquisition.

In this puzzle, discover the words related to the extraordinary adventures of Mr. Grant Money. Can you find all the hidden words that capture the essence of this remarkable story?

Now, here are the 15 words for the word search puzzle based on the story:

T	E	X	C	E	L	L	E	N	C	E	N	A	C
R	A	X	O	I	T	A	I	O	T	T	O	I	I
A	Z	E	M	D	N	R	E	A	U	M	I	Y	N
N	Y	X	P	O	A	I	S	U	I	T	T	N	I
S	C	P	E	S	T	Z	T	S	A	I	A	E	N
F	A	E	T	C	L	O	M	U	N	T	T	S	N
O	M	R	I	T	U	N	E	U	Y	S	U	T	O
R	O	T	T	P	S	A	M	C	N	I	P	L	V
M	L	I	I	L	N	M	I	I	I	A	E	U	A
A	P	S	O	N	O	C	F	C	O	S	R	S	T
T	I	E	N	C	C	P	E	A	E	N	C	E	I
I	D	P	I	H	S	R	E	D	A	E	L	R	O
O	A	E	O	S	U	C	C	E	S	S	E	R	N
N	U	U	N	I	T	E	D	T	N	A	R	G	R

CONSULTANT
TRANSFORMATION
INNOVATION
SUCCESS
COMMUNITY
RESULTS
UNITED
DIPLOMACY
ARIZONA
EXPERTISE
GRANT
COMPETITION
EXCELLENCE
LEADERSHIP
REPUTATION

GRANT CENTRAL USA

"While the grant acquisition world often witnesses fierce competition and cutthroat tactics, the legend of Mr. Grant Money reminds us that the path to true success lies in integrity, unity, and unwavering commitment to the greater good."

The Amazing Adventures of MR GRANT MONEY

STYLE & SUBSTANCE

Style and Substance: Mr. Grant Money's Graceful Journey

The Art of Grant Acquisition, Charm, and Elegance Unveiled

Mr. Grant Money was not just a master of grant acquisition; he was also a master of style. It was a sunny morning, and he was sitting in the elegant lobby of a prestigious hotel, dressed impeccably from head to toe. His customized embroidered shirt, Italian shoes, finely crafted hat, and signature cologne exuded an air of sophistication that turned heads wherever he went.

As he sipped on his tea, a lady seated nearby couldn't help but notice his aura of elegance and style. Her curiosity piqued, she decided to strike up a conversation. "Excuse me," she said, her eyes scanning Mr. Grant Money's attire. "You look absolutely impeccable. May I ask who you are and what you do?"

Mr. Grant Money, always the embodiment of charm and elegance, flashed a charismatic smile and replied, "Why, my dear, I am Mr. Grant Money, a Master Grant Acquisition Specialist. I help organizations secure the funding they need to turn their dreams into reality."

The lady's interest was piqued, and she leaned in, eager to learn more. "Master Grant Acquisition Specialist? That sounds fascinating. Could you tell me more about what that entails?"

Mr. Grant Money, with a twinkle in his eye, began to share stories of his adventures in the world of grants. He spoke of struggling nonprofits in Chicago, a school district in New York, and government departments in Arizona, all of whom had experienced remarkable transformations under his guidance. He painted a vivid picture of how his intelligence, charm, and expertise had turned their financial woes into success stories.

As he spoke, the lady's eyes lit up with excitement. She couldn't help but think of other cities and nonprofits that could benefit from Mr. Grant Money's magic touch. She leaned forward and said,

"This is incredible! I know of so many organizations that could use your help. How can they get in touch with you?"

Mr. Grant Money, always gracious, reached into his pocket and handed her a business card. "You can find me at GrantAcquisition.com," he said, his voice dripping with elegance. "But I must warn you, my dear, my waiting list is quite long, and my fees are high. However, I assure you, I'm worth every penny and more."

He paused, allowing the lady to absorb his words before adding, "You see, my goal is not just to secure grants. It's to transform organizations and communities, to leave a lasting legacy of success. And that, my dear, is a journey that requires patience, dedication, and a touch of style."

With that, Mr. Grant Money bid the lady farewell and disappeared into the hotel's opulent surroundings, leaving her with a sense of wonder and the knowledge that she had encountered a true master of his craft. As for his next destination, it remained a tantalizing mystery, but one thing was certain: wherever Mr. Grant Money went, he brought with him the promise of transformation and financial success.

Exercise: "The Style and Substance Workshop"

In the spirit of Mr. Grant Money's elegance, charm, and ability to engage others, this exercise focuses on improving your ability to make a memorable and sophisticated impression in professional interactions, whether for grant acquisition or other endeavors.

Objective: Learn the art of style and substance in professional interactions, making a positive and lasting impression in your career and networking efforts.

Steps:

1. Image and Style Analysis:
- Reflect on your personal style and image in professional settings. Consider your clothing, grooming, and overall presentation. What impression does your style currently convey?

2. Define Your Personal Brand:
- Identify the key qualities or attributes you want to be known for in your professional life. Is it confidence, expertise, charm, or sophistication?

3. Upgrade Your Wardrobe:
- Invest in a few key clothing items or accessories that align with the image you want to project. This might include a well-tailored suit, stylish shoes, or signature accessories.

4. Grooming and Self-Care:
- Pay attention to grooming and self-care practices that enhance your appearance and self-confidence. This might include skincare routines, haircare, or regular fitness activities.

5. Networking Etiquette:
- Study and practice professional networking etiquette, including how to initiate and engage in conversations, follow up with contacts, and leave a lasting impression.

6. Storytelling Practice:
- Craft and practice personal or professional stories that convey your expertise, charm, and accomplishments. These stories should be engaging and memorable.

7. Engage in Mock Conversations:
- Partner with a colleague, mentor, or friend to engage in mock networking conversations. Practice the art of gracious, engaging, and elegant communication.

8. Business Card Design:

- If you don't already have one, create a professional business card that reflects your personal brand. Ensure it includes your contact information and a brief tagline about your expertise

9. Online Presence:

- Review and update your professional online presence, including your LinkedIn profile and any other relevant social media profiles. Ensure they align with the image you want to convey.

10. Elevator Pitch:

- Craft a succinct and engaging elevator pitch that highlights your expertise and what you bring to professional relationships.

11. Role-Playing:

- Engage in role-playing exercises where you practice meeting new people in a variety of professional settings, such as conferences, networking events, or business meetings.

12. Seek Feedback:

- Request feedback from mentors, colleagues, or friends about the improvements you've made and the impact on your professional interactions.

This exercise is about developing a style and substance that make you memorable and approachable in professional settings. By practicing the art of charm and sophistication, you can enhance your networking skills and leave a lasting impression on those you meet, just as Mr. Grant Money did in the story.

> "In the world of grant acquisition, my style isn't just about impeccable attire; it's about crafting success with intelligence and charm. I don't secure grants; I create legacies of transformation and financial elegance."
> -Mr. Grant Money

Discussion Questions

1. Mr. Grant Money is portrayed as a master of both grant acquisition and style. How does his impeccable attire and charismatic demeanor contribute to his success as a grant consultant, and what role does personal presentation play in the world of grant acquisition and consulting?

2. The story highlights Mr. Grant Money's ability to leave a lasting legacy of success. What specific examples or aspects of his work suggest that he goes beyond securing grants and truly transforms organizations and communities?

3. Mr. Grant Money mentions that his waiting list is long and his fees are high. What qualities or expertise do you think set him apart from other grant consultants that make organizations willing to invest in his services, and what potential benefits might justify his fees?

4. The story portrays an encounter between Mr. Grant Money and a lady who becomes intrigued by his work. What lessons can individuals or organizations take from this interaction in terms of recognizing the value of expert consultants and seeking out their services?

5. Mr. Grant Money is described as leaving behind a promise of transformation and financial success wherever he goes. What do you think are the key principles or strategies that underlie his ability to consistently deliver successful outcomes, and how can other grant consultants or organizations learn from his approach?

💡 Big Idea "Elegance in Business Seminars"

Inspired by Mr. Grant Money's style and the charm he brought to his profession, a series of "Elegance in Business Seminars" could be established. These seminars would focus on the art of combining professional expertise with personal style, fostering a culture of grace, charm, and excellence in business.

Business leaders, entrepreneurs, and professionals from various industries could attend these seminars to learn not only about grant acquisition but also about the significance of personal branding, communication, and networking in their success. These seminars would promote a holistic approach to business, emphasizing the impact of one's demeanor, style, and presentation in achieving professional goals.

🔍 Word Search

Welcome to the world of Mr. Grant Money, the master of both grants and style. In this exciting word search puzzle, we invite you to explore the elegance and sophistication that define Mr. Grant Money's persona. Discover 15 words hidden within this puzzle that capture his impeccable fashion sense, charismatic charm, and extraordinary journey through the realm of grant acquisition.

In this puzzle, discover the words related to the extraordinary adventures of Mr. Grant Money. Can you find all the hidden words that capture the essence of this remarkable story?

Now, here are the 15 words for the word search puzzle based on the story:

S	E	L	W	I	T	N	N	E	N	Y	G	R	E
M	E	O	A	G	R	I	O	M	I	S	L	C	N
S	I	R	I	S	A	C	I	B	E	U	T	I	C
P	M	G	T	I	N	H	T	R	L	C	I	O	A
E	P	A	I	I	S	A	A	O	E	C	T	S	S
C	E	N	N	I	F	R	C	I	G	E	A	E	E
I	C	I	G	E	O	I	I	D	A	S	L	O	L
A	C	Z	L	C	R	S	T	E	N	S	I	S	Y
L	A	A	I	O	M	M	S	R	C	O	A	E	T
I	B	T	S	L	A	A	I	E	E	E	N	E	S
S	L	I	T	O	T	T	H	D	A	L	E	F	A
T	E	O	E	G	I	I	P	A	A	P	A	S	I
N	I	N	M	N	O	C	O	Y	C	A	G	E	L
I	H	S	M	E	N	G	S	O	E	E	I	P	M

SPECIALIST
TRANSFORMATION
ORGANIZATIONS
SUCCESS
SOPHISTICATION
COLOGNE
LEGACY
EMBROIDERED
CHARISMATIC
IMPECCABLE
WAITING LIST
STYLE
FEES
ELEGANCE
ITALIAN

"Amid the hustle and bustle of life, Mr. Grant Money's aura of sophistication and charm reminds us that success isn't just about what you do but how you do it. His story is a testament to the power of grace and style, both in attire and in the pursuit of transformative achievements."

SWAY TO SUCCESS

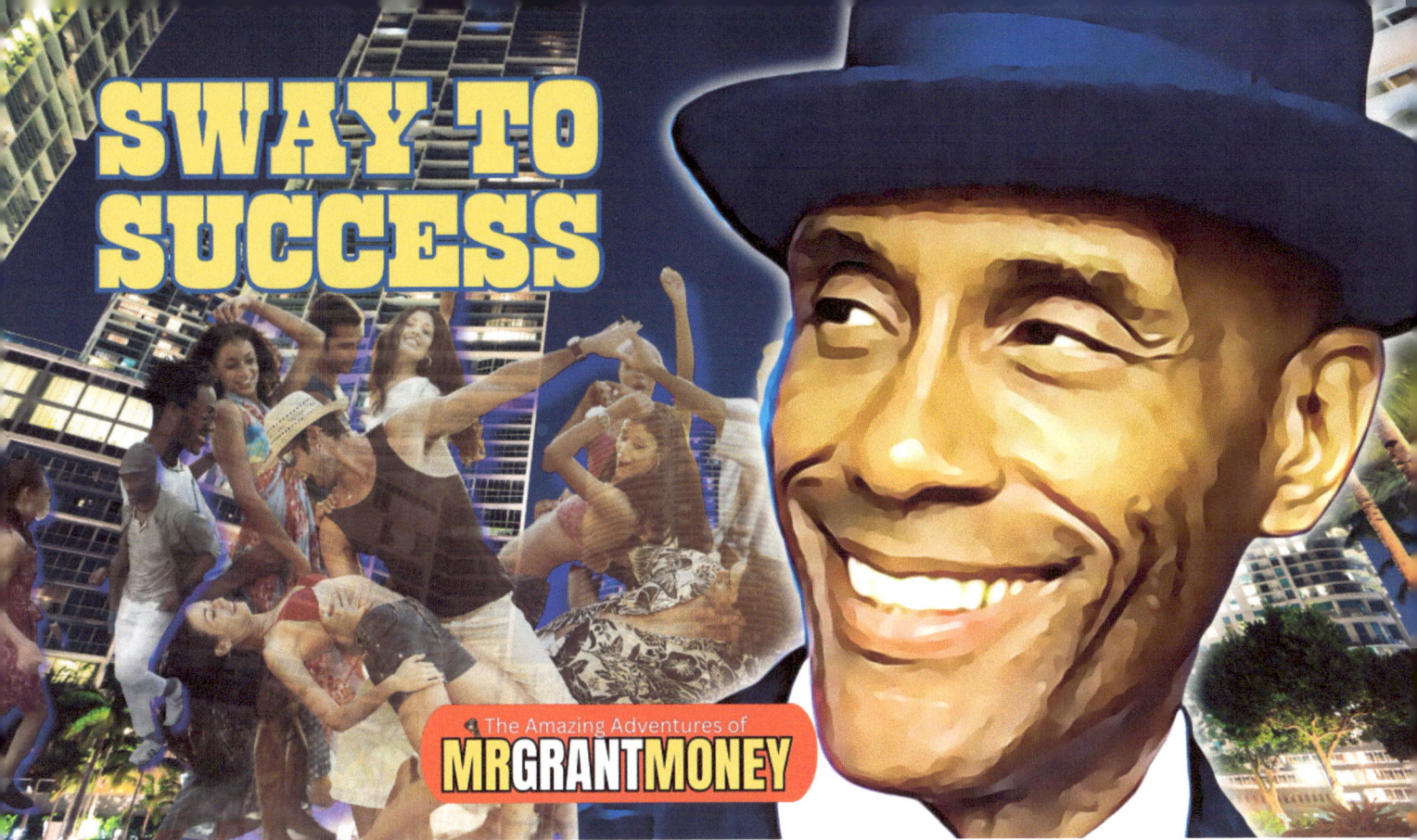

The Amazing Adventures of
MRGRANTMONEY

Swaying to Success: Mr. Grant Money's Miami Rendezvous

When Elegance on the Dance Floor Meets Grant Acquisition Brilliance

After a string of successful grant-acquisition adventures, Mr. Grant Money decided to take a well-deserved break in the vibrant city of Miami. He checked into a luxurious hotel and looked forward to some rest and relaxation under the warm Florida sun.

One evening, as he strolled along the lively streets of Miami, he stumbled upon a hot salsa party. The energetic music and the passionate dance moves of the revelers drew him in, and he couldn't resist joining the festivities. Mr. Grant Money, known for his elegant style and charm, soon found himself effortlessly gliding across the dance floor, captivating everyone with his moves.

It was a sight to behold, and the crowd couldn't take their eyes off him. Mr. Grant Money, though not intentionally trying to steal the spotlight, had become the center of attention. He danced only once that night, but his elegance left an indelible mark.

As he caught his breath, a business executive and his partner approached him, their admiration evident in their eyes. "Excuse me," the executive said, "aren't you Mr. Grant Money? We've seen your training videos on YouTube."

Mr. Grant Money smiled graciously and acknowledged his identity. "Indeed, I am. It's a pleasure to meet you both."

The couple was still in awe of his dancing prowess, and the executive couldn't help but express his surprise. "We had no idea you could dance so well, Mr. Grant Money. It's truly impressive."

Mr. Grant Money, oozing confidence, saw an opportunity to turn this moment into a teaching experience. He explained, "Dancing, much like grant acquisition, requires finesse, partnership, and a shared rhythm. Just as in dancing, when applying for grants, you must understand the needs and expectations of the funding organizations, find the right partner, and move in harmony to achieve success."

The couple listened with amazement, realizing that one of Mr. Grant Money's points directly addressed a critical issue they were facing in their business. They exchanged glances, their desire to become clients of Mr. Grant Money unmistakable.

With a self-assured elegance, Mr. Grant Money graciously accepted their interest but then delivered the news with a touch of elegance, "I appreciate your interest, but I'm currently at full capacity and not accepting new clients at the moment. However, you can get in line, and when the time is right, we can explore how I can assist you."

The couple nodded in understanding, knowing that the opportunity to work with Mr. Grant Money would be well worth the wait.

As the salsa party continued to pulse with energy, Mr. Grant Money bid the couple farewell and vanished into the Miami night, his next destination a tantalizing mystery. Wherever he went, one thing was certain: whether dancing or acquiring grants, Mr. Grant Money's elegance, charm, and wisdom always left an unforgettable impression.

Exercise: "The Dance of Grant Acquisition"

In the story of Mr. Grant Money's Miami adventure, we see the parallel between dancing and grant acquisition, emphasizing the importance of finesse, partnership, and a shared rhythm. This exercise aims to help you understand and internalize these principles, making your grant acquisition efforts more successful.

Objective: To practice and refine your grant acquisition skills by applying dance-related concepts.

Steps:

1. Identify a Grant Opportunity:
- Start by researching and identifying a grant opportunity that aligns with your organization's goals or projects. This will be your "dance partner" for this exercise.

2. Learn the "Dance Steps":
- Study the grant application guidelines, eligibility criteria, and requirements thoroughly. Just as in dance, you need to understand the rhythm and steps before you hit the floor.

3. Find Your "Dance Partner":
- In the story, Mr. Grant Money emphasized the importance of the right partnership. In grant acquisition, this means finding collaborators, advisors, or consultants who can help you strengthen your application. Identify individuals or organizations with expertise in your field who can support your grant-seeking efforts.

4. Coordinate Your Moves:
- Much like dancing in harmony with a partner, your grant application should align with the goals and priorities of the funding organization. Tailor your proposal to demonstrate that you and the funding source share the same rhythm and goals.

5. Dress for Success:
- Just as Mr. Grant Money oozed elegance on the dance floor, your grant proposal should be professionally presented. Ensure that your writing is clear, concise, and free of errors. Your application should be visually appealing and well-organized.

6. Seek Feedback:
- Before submitting your grant proposal, share it with trusted colleagues, mentors, or advisors. Their feedback can help you refine your "dance moves" and make your application more appealing.

7. Apply with Confidence:
- Submit your grant application with confidence, knowing that you've prepared thoroughly, just like Mr. Grant Money's elegant dance moves. Remember the importance of self-assurance in the grant acquisition process.

8. Network and Build Relationships:
- In the story, Mr. Grant Money was recognized because of his YouTube videos. In your grant-seeking journey, consider building an online presence or attending networking events to create visibility and relationships in the grant community.

9. Be Patient:
- As Mr. Grant Money advised, sometimes, you may not be able to accept all opportunities at once. If you don't secure the grant immediately, be patient and keep the possibility of future collaboration in mind.

10. Reflect and Adjust:
- After the grant application process, whether you succeed or not, take time to reflect on what worked well and what could be improved. This reflection will help you refine your "dance moves" for future grant opportunities.

Remember that grant acquisition is a process that can require time and perseverance. Just like a dancer who practices to improve their skills, your grant-seeking abilities will improve with experience and dedication. So, keep dancing and refining your steps in the world of grant acquisition.

> "In the dance of life, whether on the ballroom floor or in the world of grants, success is about finding the right partner, understanding their rhythm, and moving in harmony to achieve greatness."
> -Mr. Grant Money

Discussion Questions

1. The story draws a parallel between dancing and grant acquisition, emphasizing the need for finesse, partnership, and shared rhythm. How can organizations apply the lessons from dancing to their grant acquisition strategies, and what specific examples can demonstrate the importance of understanding the needs and expectations of funding organizations and finding the right partners?

2. Mr. Grant Money's dancing prowess unexpectedly led to a conversation about grant acquisition, highlighting the intersection of his two talents. What aspects of his explanation about grant acquisition resonated with the business executive and his partner, and how might other organizations adapt their approaches based on this conversation?

3. The story mentions that Mr. Grant Money was not accepting new clients at the moment but suggested that the couple get in line. How can organizations prepare themselves to be in a strong position when the time is right to seek expert grant acquisition assistance, and what qualities or attributes might make them more appealing to consultants like Mr. Grant Money?

4. The story emphasizes that Mr. Grant Money's elegance, charm, and wisdom always leave an unforgettable impression. What are the key attributes that contribute to his success and make him a sought-after consultant in the field of grant acquisition, and how can other organizations and grant seekers incorporate similar qualities into their strategies?

5. Mr. Grant Money's next destination remains a mystery. What do you think is the key to his enduring appeal and success, and how can organizations proactively position themselves to benefit from his expertise when he arrives in their area or becomes available to take on new clients?

💡 **Big Idea** "Elegance in Leadership Workshops"

Inspired by Mr. Grant Money's ability to draw parallels between dancing and grant acquisition, Miami could create a program called "Elegance in Leadership Workshops." These workshops would blend elements of dance and leadership, using dance as a metaphor for leadership principles. Participants would learn how to lead with finesse, develop effective partnerships, and work in harmony with their teams, just as Mr. Grant Money described. The program would cater to business executives, community leaders, and nonprofit managers, helping them enhance their leadership skills in a unique and engaging way. By embracing the elegance of dance, these workshops would create more effective and charismatic leaders in Miami, fostering better collaboration and success.

🔍 Word Search

Step into the enchanting world of Mr. Grant Money, the master of both grant acquisition and elegant dance. In this captivating word search puzzle, we invite you to uncover the hidden words that capture the essence of his graceful style, his charm, and the unique experiences he encounters on his adventures.

In this puzzle, discover the words related to the extraordinary adventures of Mr. Grant Money. Can you find all the hidden words that capture the essence of this remarkable story?

Now, here are the 15 words for the word search puzzle based on the story:

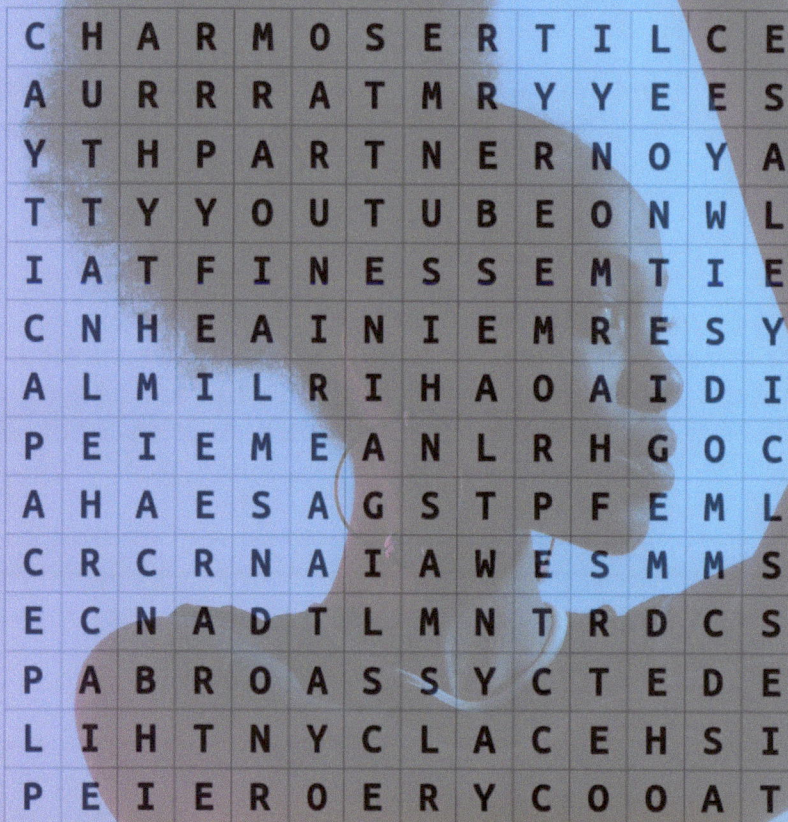

C	H	A	R	M	O	S	E	R	T	I	L	C	E
A	U	R	R	R	A	T	M	R	Y	Y	E	E	S
Y	T	H	P	A	R	T	N	E	R	N	O	Y	A
T	T	Y	Y	O	U	T	U	B	E	O	N	W	L
I	A	T	F	I	N	E	S	S	E	M	T	I	E
C	N	H	E	A	I	N	I	E	M	R	E	S	Y
A	L	M	I	L	R	I	H	A	O	A	I	D	I
P	E	I	E	M	E	A	N	L	R	H	G	O	C
A	H	A	E	S	A	G	S	T	P	F	E	M	L
C	R	C	R	N	A	I	A	W	E	S	M	M	S
E	C	N	A	D	T	L	M	N	T	R	D	C	S
P	A	B	R	O	A	S	S	Y	C	T	E	D	E
L	I	H	T	N	Y	C	L	A	C	E	H	S	I
P	E	I	E	R	O	E	R	Y	C	O	O	A	T

SALSA
HARMONY
FINESSE
STYLE
MIAMI
WISDOM
YOUTUBE
RHYTHM
CHARM
DANCE
ELEGANCE
INTEREST
CAPACITY
CLIENTS
PARTNER

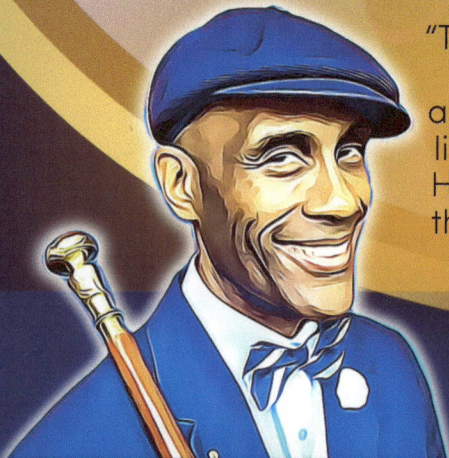

"The chance encounter with Mr. Grant Money at a salsa party serves as a reminder that success is not only about professional expertise but also about embracing life's unexpected moments with grace and enthusiasm. His dance moves left an impact that extended beyond the dance floor, offering a valuable lesson in the art of seizing opportunities."

From Novice to Maestro: Mr. Grant Money's Reflective Journey

The Humble Origins and Grand Achievements of a Grant Acquisition Guru

Mr. Grant Money relaxed in the intense heat of the sauna, beads of sweat glistened on his forehead. The warmth enveloped him, and he let his mind wander back to the early days of his career as a novice grant writer. It seemed like a lifetime ago when he was just starting out, learning the ropes of the grant acquisition world.

With a reflective smile, he whispered to himself, "I've come a long way. Who would have thought that my humble beginnings would snowball into over half a billion dollars garnered by government agencies and nonprofits, thanks in part to my guidance and insight imparted to countless thousands?"

As the heat penetrated his skin, Mr. Grant Money's thoughts continued to drift. He contemplated the transformative power of vision and action. He pondered aloud, "I wonder how many other nonprofits and organizations could benefit from simply learning to slow down, think, and envision a brighter future. What would happen if they wrote down their aspirations and beliefs, and then backed them up with concrete action? Our world would be different, and more grants would be secured."

With renewed purpose and a sense of fulfillment, Mr. Grant Money rose from the sauna, feeling invigorated and ready for his next challenge. He knew that there were countless organizations out there in need of his expertise, and he was eager to guide them towards success.

As he dried off and dressed in his signature elegant style, he sat down at his desk and pulled out a list of those who had placed a $5,000 deposit to potentially become his coveted clients. Cherry-picking through the list, he meticulously reviewed each applicant's needs and potential for impact.

Mr. Grant Money understood that his time and expertise were in high demand, and he took his role as a grant acquisition specialist seriously. He was selective about who he chose to work with, ensuring that his clients were not only in need of funding but also committed to making a positive change in their communities.

With his next challenge on the horizon, Mr. Grant Money couldn't help but feel a sense of excitement and anticipation. He knew that every new adventure brought with it the opportunity to transform lives and make a difference in the world of grant acquisition.

And so, with his client list carefully curated, Mr. Grant Money embarked on his next journey, ready to help organizations secure the funding they needed to turn their visions into reality. As he left his office, the words of his earlier reflection echoed in his mind, reminding him of the powerful impact that vision, belief, and action could have on the world.

Exercise: "Vision to Action: Charting Your Grant Acquisition Journey"

The story of Mr. Grant Money's reflective journey emphasizes the transformative power of vision and action in the grant acquisition world. This exercise will help you or your participants learn how to set clear goals and take actionable steps to achieve success in grant acquisition.

Objective: To help individuals set clear goals and take concrete steps to improve their grant acquisition skills and increase their chances of securing grants for their organizations or projects.

Steps:

1. Identify Your Vision:
- Take some time to reflect on your grant acquisition goals and the impact you want to make. What is the vision for your organization or project? What positive changes do you want to bring to your community or field? Write down your vision statement.

2. Set Specific Grant Acquisition Goals:
- Based on your vision, break down your goals into specific, measurable, achievable, relevant, and time-bound (SMART) objectives. For example, specify the number of grants you want to apply for, the amount of funding you aim to secure, and the impact you want to achieve within a certain timeframe.

3. Prioritize Your Target Grants:
- Just as Mr. Grant Money carefully reviewed each potential client's needs, prioritize the grants that align most closely with your vision and goals. Research grant opportunities and create a list of those you plan to pursue.

4. Create an Action Plan:
- Develop a detailed action plan that outlines the steps you need to take to achieve your grant acquisition goals. Include deadlines, responsibilities, and specific tasks, such as researching grants, drafting proposals, and building relationships with funders.

5. Commit to Action:
- As Mr. Grant Money was committed to helping organizations, commit to taking action to realize your grant acquisition goals. Make a pledge to yourself or within your organization to stay focused and dedicated to the plan you've created.

6. Implement the Action Plan:

- Begin executing the tasks outlined in your action plan. Start by researching grants, gathering required documents, and drafting proposals. Monitor your progress and make adjustments as needed.

7. Reflect and Adjust:

- Periodically review your progress and assess whether you're on track to achieve your grant acquisition goals. If necessary, make adjustments to your action plan to address any challenges or changes in your organization's needs.

8. Network and Seek Expertise:

- Just as Mr. Grant Money used his expertise to help organizations, seek out mentorship or guidance from grant professionals who can provide valuable insights and advice. Building a network of contacts in the grant acquisition field can also be beneficial.

9. Stay Selective and Committed:

- Remember Mr. Grant Money's selective approach to choosing clients. Continue to prioritize grant opportunities that align with your organization's mission and commitment to making a positive impact in your community.

10. Celebrate Achievements:

- As you achieve milestones and secure grants, take time to celebrate your successes and acknowledge the progress you've made toward your vision. Recognize the difference you're making in your community or field.

By following these steps, individuals or organizations can transform their grant acquisition journey from a mere vision into actionable plans and concrete achievements, just as Mr. Grant Money did in his reflective journey.

> "From humble beginnings to the pinnacle of grant acquisition, my journey has been a testament to the transformative power of vision and action. Every step, every grant, has shaped a brighter future for countless communities."
> -Mr. Grant Money

Discussion Questions

1. Mr. Grant Money reflects on the transformative power of vision and action in his career. How do his thoughts on slowing down, envisioning a brighter future, and backing up aspirations with concrete action apply to organizations seeking grant funding, and what strategies can they use to align their goals with potential grant opportunities?

2. The story mentions Mr. Grant Money's selectivity in choosing clients who are not only in need of funding but also committed to making a positive change in their communities. How can organizations demonstrate their commitment and readiness to work with grant consultants effectively, and what qualities or attributes might make them more appealing to experts like Mr. Grant Money?

3. The narrative suggests that Mr. Grant Money has helped secure over half a billion dollars for government agencies and nonprofits. Can you provide examples or insights into the specific strategies or approaches he has used to achieve this remarkable level of success in the world of grant acquisition?

4. Mr. Grant Money's story emphasizes his renewed sense of purpose and excitement for each new challenge. What lessons can organizations draw from his dedication and passion for helping them secure funding, and how can they maintain enthusiasm and commitment throughout the grant acquisition process?

5. The story highlights Mr. Grant Money's reflection on his career journey. How can other grant acquisition professionals or organizations benefit from reflecting on their experiences and achievements, and what strategies can they use to continuously improve and make a lasting impact in the field of grant acquisition?

💡 Big Idea "Grant Visionaries' Retreat"

In light of Mr. Grant Money's reflective journey, the concept of a "Grant Visionaries' Retreat" could be created. This retreat would provide a space for nonprofit leaders, government officials, and aspiring grant writers to slow down, reflect, and develop a clear vision for their organizations.

During the retreat, participants would learn about the power of articulating their goals and beliefs and then back them up with concrete action plans. They would receive guidance on grant acquisition strategies and have the opportunity to work on their grant proposals in a serene and focused environment. The "Grant Visionaries' Retreat" would foster a culture of thoughtful, vision-driven leadership, helping organizations secure the funding needed to turn their aspirations into reality.

🔍 Word Search

Join us in delving into the remarkable journey of Mr. Grant Money, a true legend in the world of grant acquisition. In this word search puzzle, we invite you to discover hidden words that encapsulate the essence of Mr. Grant Money's journey, from his early days as a novice grant writer to his impressive achievements in guiding government agencies and nonprofits to secure over half a billion dollars in funding.

In this puzzle, discover the words related to the extraordinary adventures of Mr. Grant Money. Can you find all the hidden words that capture the essence of this remarkable story?

Now, here are the 14 words for the word search puzzle based on the story:

N	T	S	R	A	C	A	C	T	I	S	A	V	O
N	E	E	I	L	C	H	A	L	L	E	N	G	E
V	A	S	N	O	I	T	A	R	I	P	S	A	E
B	R	T	T	E	T	I	I	O	T	E	T	C	P
E	F	U	N	D	I	N	G	O	S	X	N	N	I
L	E	S	E	I	S	S	E	I	N	P	E	T	G
I	P	I	N	I	N	I	S	S	G	E	C	V	S
E	C	N	O	N	E	G	E	S	I	R	N	I	E
F	B	M	N	P	F	H	N	T	N	T	A	S	O
S	N	I	U	T	P	T	O	N	E	I	D	I	L
V	I	M	P	A	C	T	V	A	G	S	I	O	G
O	U	T	C	U	I	B	I	R	I	E	U	N	I
I	N	I	A	A	X	O	C	G	S	D	G	T	E
E	C	A	R	E	E	R	E	S	G	H	E	P	R

BELIEFS
INSIGHT
ACTION
CLIENTS
GRANT
CAREER
NOVICE
VISION
FUNDING
IMPACT
GUIDANCE
EXPERTISE
CHALLENGE
ASPIRATIONS

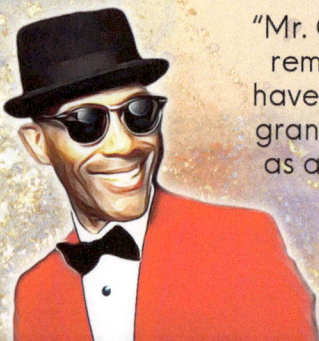

"Mr. Grant Money's reflective moment in the sauna serves as a reminder of the profound impact that vision and action can have in the world of grant acquisition. His journey, from novice grant writer to a half-billion-dollar catalyst of change, stands as a testament to the transformative power of belief, action, and unwavering dedication."

THE SEVEN PILLARS OF GRANT ACQUISITION

The Amazing Adventures of
MRGRANTMONEY

The Seven Pillars of Grant Acquisition: Mr. Grant Money's Parisian Revelation

Resizing a Pinky Ring and Refining a Strategy for Grant Funding

Mr. Grant Money, the man of elegance and style, found himself seated in the first-class section of a plane bound for Paris. He was on a mission to meet with his personal jeweler, who was going to resize his iconic pinky ring adorned with seven dazzling diamonds. The flight promised comfort and luxury, a fitting preamble to his upcoming rendezvous with the jeweler.

As he settled into his plush seat, Mr. Grant Money couldn't help but notice the airline stewardess, who was the embodiment of grace and beauty. She was clearly intrigued by the mysterious and well-dressed man seated in her section, and her curiosity got the best of her.

With a warm and inviting smile, she initiated a conversation with Mr. Grant Money. "Good day, sir," she began. "I couldn't help but notice your impeccable style. You're like a UFO— an Unidentified Fly Object— on this flight."

Mr. Grant Money, ever the gentleman, acknowledged her compliment with a nod. "Thank you, my dear. I do appreciate elegance in all aspects of life."

The stewardess, her curiosity piqued, couldn't resist dropping hints of flirtation into the conversation. She asked about his travels and personal interests, but Mr. Grant Money remained focused and professional. He knew that his client's grant acquisition plan deserved his undivided attention.

As the plane cruised at 35,000 feet, Mr. Grant Money delved into the details of the grant acquisition plan for the large international nonprofit. He meticulously reviewed every aspect, ensuring that it aligned with the organization's mission and the expectations of potential funders. His expertise and commitment to his clients were unwavering.

Finally, the plane touched down in Paris, and Mr. Grant Money disembarked with a sense of purpose. He headed straight to his jeweler's boutique, where the elegant and knowledgeable artisan greeted him with a warm embrace.

As Mr. Grant Money described his desire to resize the pinky ring with its seven exquisite diamonds, he couldn't help but draw a parallel between the gems and the pillars of success in grant acquisition. He explained, "Just as these seven diamonds symbolize the facets of brilliance, a successful grant acquisition plan relies on seven essential pillars: clear goals, strategic planning, effective storytelling, targeted research, strong relationships, flawless execution, and diligent reporting."

The jeweler, captivated by Mr. Grant Money's wisdom, began the delicate process of resizing the ring, ensuring that it would continue to grace Mr. Grant Money's hand with its elegant charm.

With the resizing completed, Mr. Grant Money left the jeweler's boutique, confident that his pinky ring now perfectly mirrored the seven pillars of success in grant acquisition. He knew that his client's grant acquisition plan was in capable hands and that he was ready to guide them towards securing the funding they needed to make a difference in the world.

As he boarded the return flight, the stewardess couldn't help but notice the slight twinkle in Mr. Grant Money's eye, a reflection of the satisfaction that came from a job well done. With elegance and style, he settled back into his first-class seat, ready to continue his amazing adventures in the world of grants.

Exercise: "The Seven Pillars of Grant Acquisition"

The story of Mr. Grant Money's seven pillars of grant acquisition highlights essential principles for success in grant funding. This exercise helps you or your participants reflect on these pillars and apply them to their own grant acquisition strategies.

Objective: To identify and reinforce the seven key pillars of successful grant acquisition in your grant-seeking efforts.

Steps:

1. Identify Your Goals (Pillar 1):
- Take a moment to clearly define your organization's or project's goals. What do you want to achieve with the grant funding? Write down specific and measurable objectives.

2. Strategic Planning (Pillar 2):
- Develop a strategic plan for your grant acquisition efforts. Consider your target funders, timelines, and resources. Create a timeline or action plan outlining your approach.

3. Effective Storytelling (Pillar 3):
- Practice the art of storytelling. Craft a compelling narrative that explains why your organization or project is deserving of grant funding. Use vivid examples and emotionally resonant language to make your case.

4. Targeted Research (Pillar 4):
- Conduct in-depth research to identify grants that align with your mission and goals. Explore online databases, grant directories, and the websites of potential funders. Make a list of relevant grants.

5. Build Strong Relationships (Pillar 5):
- Reach out to potential funders and develop relationships with them. Connect with program officers, attend networking events, and engage with grant makers to build trust and understanding.

6. Flawless Execution (Pillar 6):

- Create a detailed plan for drafting and submitting grant proposals. Follow this plan meticulously, ensuring that your applications are well-prepared, meet all requirements, and are submitted on time.

7. Diligent Reporting (Pillar 7):

- After securing grant funding, commit to thorough and timely reporting to your funders. Maintain transparency and accountability by delivering progress reports and financial statements as required.

8. Reflect on Your Grant Strategy:

- Consider how well you are currently incorporating these seven pillars into your grant acquisition process. Are there areas where you can improve or refine your approach?

9. Create Your Pillar-Driven Grant Plan:

- Develop a grant acquisition plan that explicitly addresses each of the seven pillars. Outline how you will implement each pillar in your grant-seeking efforts.

10. Execute and Review:

- Put your pillar-driven plan into action. As you work on grant applications and interactions with funders, continuously review your strategy to ensure that each pillar is being upheld.

11. Share Your Insights:

- Share your experiences and insights with peers or colleagues involved in grant acquisition. Discuss how focusing on these seven pillars has enhanced your grant-seeking effectiveness.

12. Celebrate Your Success:

- When you secure grant funding, celebrate your success and recognize how the application of the seven pillars contributed to your achievements.

By actively engaging in this exercise, you can reinforce the seven pillars of grant acquisition, making them an integral part of your grant-seeking strategy, just as Mr. Grant Money did in his Parisian adventure.

Discussion Questions

1. Mr. Grant Money draws a parallel between the seven diamonds on his pinky ring and the seven pillars of success in grant acquisition. Can you elaborate on these seven pillars and provide examples of how each one contributes to a successful grant acquisition plan?

2. The story highlights Mr. Grant Money's unwavering commitment to his client's grant acquisition plan, even while engaging in casual conversation with the airline stewardess. How can organizations and grant seekers maintain focus and professionalism when working on grant applications, and what strategies can help them balance personal interactions with the demands of the task at hand?

3. Mr. Grant Money's reflection on the seven pillars of grant acquisition suggests a deep understanding of the key components for success. How might other grant acquisition professionals or organizations benefit from this perspective, and what practical steps can they take to incorporate these pillars into their grant strategies?

4. The story portrays Mr. Grant Money's sense of satisfaction after completing a job well done. How can organizations and grant seekers measure and celebrate their own successes in grant acquisition, and what benefits can come from acknowledging and reflecting on the achievement of their grant-related goals?

5. The story hints at Mr. Grant Money's continued adventures in the world of grants. What qualities or strategies do you think contribute to his ongoing success, and how can other grant consultants and organizations proactively prepare to benefit from his expertise when they engage with him?

💡 Big Idea "Seven Pillars of Grant Success Workshop"

Inspired by Mr. Grant Money's seven pillars of grant acquisition, a "Seven Pillars of Grant Success Workshop" could be designed. This workshop would focus on teaching grant seekers the seven essential components of successful grant acquisition: clear goals, strategic planning, effective storytelling, targeted research, strong relationships, flawless execution, and diligent reporting.

Participants would learn how to incorporate these pillars into their grant acquisition strategies and proposals. The workshop could cater to individuals and organizations seeking to improve their grant acquisition skills and increase their chances of securing funding for their projects. It would be a comprehensive and hands-on learning experience led by experienced grant experts.

🔍 Word Search

Join us in a journey that combines elegance, style, and the world of grants with Mr. Grant Money. In this word search puzzle, we invite you to explore hidden words that encapsulate the essence of Mr. Grant Money's remarkable adventures. From his plush first-class flights to Paris to his iconic pinky ring adorned with seven dazzling diamonds, can you find all the words that define his wisdom, expertise, and commitment to success in grant acquisition?

In this puzzle, discover the words related to the extraordinary adventures of Mr. Grant Money. Can you find all the hidden words that capture the essence of this remarkable story?

Now, here are the 14 words for the word search puzzle based on the story:

L	R	R	N	A	Y	E	E	T	I	I	E	A	S
N	E	E	L	D	R	K	S	P	E	A	F	O	E
E	P	L	S	I	I	N	N	S	N	A	I	N	I
S	O	A	S	A	M	N	E	I	P	E	O	R	T
S	R	T	T	M	N	R	C	R	P	I	E	E	P
E	T	I	Y	O	E	O	T	A	T	E	Y	O	L
C	I	O	L	N	N	L	O	I	O	I	G	N	E
C	N	N	E	D	Q	T	S	A	I	I	N	I	K
U	G	S	S	S	E	I	P	F	G	R	A	N	T
S	P	H	N	A	U	S	J	E	W	E	L	E	R
Y	A	I	I	Q	E	X	E	C	U	T	I	O	N
W	R	P	C	A	N	E	L	E	G	A	N	C	E
R	I	A	S	T	E	W	A	R	D	E	S	S	I
E	S	I	S	E	N	O	N	P	R	O	F	I	T

PINKY
ACQUISITION
EXECUTION
NONPROFIT
STYLE
GRANT
PARIS
DIAMONDS
ELEGANCE
SUCCESS
RELATIONSHIP
JEWELER
STEWARDESS
REPORTING

"The chance encounter between Mr. Grant Money and the airline stewardess serves as a reminder that true elegance is rooted in knowledge, commitment, and a focused sense of purpose. Mr. Grant Money's pinky ring and the seven pillars of grant acquisition reflect the essence of excellence and expertise in his remarkable journey to empower organizations and secure their funding needs."

Unlocking Grants: Marilyn's Journey with Mr. Grant Money's Guide

A Budget-Friendly Path to a Quarter-Million Dollar Grant Success

Marilyn Crawford, a dedicated member of her local PTA, had a dream to secure much-needed funds for her school. She had heard about the legendary Mr. Grant Money and his remarkable ability to secure grants, but with a limited budget, affording his hefty fees was out of the question. Undeterred, Marilyn decided to take matters into her own hands and explore other options.

She learned about Mr. Grant Money's Grant Acquisition Success Guide, priced at $4,997. While it was a significant investment for her, she knew it was the next best thing to having him in person. She believed that the insights she could glean from the guide would empower her and her team to take action.

As Marilyn delved into the guide, she discovered five key takeaways that would shape her grant acquisition journey:

1. The Power of Vision:
Mr. Grant Money emphasized the importance of having a clear vision for the future. Marilyn realized that by envisioning a brighter educational landscape for her school and community, she could inspire others to join her cause.

2. Effective Storytelling:

Mr. Grant Money stressed the impact of compelling storytelling. Marilyn learned to craft narratives that tugged at the heartstrings of potential funders, making her cause more relatable and compelling.

3. Strategic Partnerships:

Mr. Grant Money's guide highlighted the value of partnerships. Marilyn realized that by collaborating with her city, two other nonprofits in her area, and the school district, she could pool resources and increase their chances of securing larger grants.

4. Targeted Research:

The guide emphasized the importance of thorough research. Marilyn and her team became experts in identifying potential grant opportunities and tailoring their proposals to meet the specific criteria of each funding organization.

5. Diligence and Perseverance:

Above all, Mr. Grant Money stressed the importance of diligence and perseverance. Marilyn and her team approached their grant acquisition efforts with unwavering determination.

Using the insights, inspiration, and style she gleaned from Mr. Grant Money's guide, Marilyn embarked on a journey of grant acquisition. She forged strong partnerships with her city, the nonprofits, and the school district, aligning their goals and visions. Together, they developed a comprehensive grant proposal that aimed to enhance educational opportunities and community development.

Months of hard work paid off when they secured a quarter of a million dollar grant, exceeding their expectations. The funding would be used to improve school facilities, provide educational resources, and create a more vibrant and inclusive community.

"Empowerment knows no budget. In the world of grants, it's not the size of your wallet but the size of your vision that truly matters. Marilyn's story proves that determination and strategic insights can lead to remarkable success."
-Mr. Grant Money

Overwhelmed with gratitude, Marilyn decided to write a heartfelt thank-you note to Mr. Grant Money:

Dear Mr. Grant Money,

I wanted to express my deepest gratitude for the guidance and inspiration your Grant Acquisition Success Guide provided. Your invaluable insights empowered us to transform our dreams into reality. Thanks to your wisdom, we secured a quarter of a million dollars in grant funding, which will have a profound impact on our school and community.

The funding will enhance educational opportunities for our students, create a more inclusive environment, and contribute to the betterment of our city. Your influence, though distant, has left an indelible mark on our journey, and we couldn't be more thankful.

With warm regards and heartfelt appreciation,

Marilyn Crawford
and the entire PTA team

Though Marilyn had never met Mr. Grant Money in person, his expertise and guidance had made a world of difference. Her journey had proven that with the right vision, inspiration, and a strategic approach, remarkable achievements were possible, even without the hefty fees and first-class accommodations of a legendary grant acquisition specialist.

"Marilyn's journey exemplifies that the heart of grant acquisition isn't about the price tag—it's about the power of vision, the impact of compelling storytelling, the strength of partnerships, the importance of research, and the unwavering commitment to make a difference."
-Mr. Grant Money

Exercise: "The Grant Acquisition Power of Vision and Partnership"

Marilyn's journey to secure a quarter-million-dollar grant showcases the importance of having a clear vision and building strategic partnerships in the grant acquisition process. This exercise focuses on developing a vision and initiating steps to forge partnerships that can enhance your grant acquisition efforts, even on a limited budget.

Objective: To help individuals or organizations define a clear vision and take the initial steps to establish strategic partnerships for grant acquisition.

Steps:

1. Define Your Vision (Power of Vision):
- Take time to articulate your vision for the project or organization that requires grant funding. What impact do you want to make? What changes do you hope to see in your community or field? Write down a clear and inspiring vision statement.

2. Identify Potential Partners (Strategic Partnerships):
- Research and identify potential partners who share your vision or have complementary goals. Consider other organizations, schools, community groups, local government agencies, or individuals who may be interested in collaborating on grant applications.

3. Engage in Vision-Driven Conversations:
- Reach out to potential partners and initiate conversations about your shared vision and goals. Share your vision statement with them and inquire about their thoughts and interests. Discuss how your collaboration could lead to greater impact.

4. Craft Compelling Narratives (Effective Storytelling):
- Practice crafting compelling narratives that communicate the importance of your shared vision. Create a brief story or presentation that can be used when approaching potential partners, funders, or in grant proposals to illustrate the impact you hope to achieve.

5. Plan a Vision Workshop:
- Organize a workshop or meeting where you and your potential partners can collaboratively refine and expand upon your shared vision. Invite all stakeholders to participate and contribute their ideas, experiences, and expertise.

6. Identify Common Objectives:
- During the vision workshop, identify common objectives and goals that can serve as a foundation for grant proposals. Discuss how your combined efforts can enhance your chances of securing funding.

7. Strategize Resource Pooling (Strategic Partnerships):
- Explore opportunities to pool resources, whether it's human resources, expertise, or financial contributions. Define roles and responsibilities for each partner in the grant acquisition process.

8. Begin Targeted Research (Targeted Research):
- As a group, conduct research to identify grant opportunities that align with your shared vision and objectives. Each partner can take on specific tasks related to researching potential funders and grant opportunities.

9. Build a Partnership Proposal:
- Collaboratively draft a partnership proposal outlining the vision, goals, resources, and commitment of each partner. This document can be shared with potential funders and grant-making organizations.

10. Take the First Steps:
- Begin reaching out to funders and applying for grants, emphasizing the strength of your partnership and the collective impact you aim to achieve.

11. Regularly Review and Refine:
- Continuously meet with your partners to review progress and adjust your strategies as needed. Keep the lines of communication open and maintain a commitment to achieving your shared vision.

12. Celebrate Achievements and Express Gratitude:
- As you secure grants and make progress toward your vision, celebrate your achievements with your partners. Express gratitude for their collaboration and support.

By engaging in this exercise, you can harness the power of vision and partnerships to enhance your grant acquisition efforts, just as Marilyn did to secure a quarter-million-dollar grant for her school and community.

Discussion Questions

1. Marilyn's story highlights her journey to secure a quarter-million dollar grant using Mr. Grant Money's guide. Can you provide examples or insights into how each of the five key takeaways she gleaned from the guide—vision, storytelling, partnerships, targeted research, and diligence—contributed to her grant acquisition success, and how can organizations apply these principles to their own grant-seeking efforts?

2. The story emphasizes Marilyn's determination to explore budget-friendly options for grant acquisition, such as using Mr. Grant Money's guide. How can organizations with limited resources identify cost-effective strategies and resources to improve their grant acquisition efforts, and what other accessible tools or guides might be available to assist them?

3. Marilyn expresses her gratitude to Mr. Grant Money for his guidance and inspiration. What are the potential benefits of acknowledging the influence of mentors, guides, or experts in the field of grant acquisition, and how can organizations and grant seekers effectively express their appreciation to those who have helped them achieve success?

4. The story showcases the impact of Marilyn's grant acquisition journey on her school and community. What are the long-term implications and potential ripple effects of successful grant acquisition, and how can organizations leverage their achievements to create lasting positive change within their communities?

5. Mr. Grant Money's guide played a pivotal role in Marilyn's success. How can organizations and individuals assess the credibility and quality of grant acquisition guides or resources to ensure that they are making informed and valuable investments in their grant-seeking efforts?

💡 **Big Idea** "Empowerment Grants"

Inspired by Marilyn's journey and the impact of Mr. Grant Money's guide, a program called "Empowerment Grants" could be established. These grants would provide financial support to individuals, nonprofit organizations, and community groups seeking to access resources, training, and tools that empower them to take control of their own grant acquisition efforts. The grants could cover the cost of grant acquisition guides, training programs, or consultation fees from grant specialists.

The goal of the "Empowerment Grants" would be to level the playing field, allowing more individuals and organizations with limited budgets to access the knowledge and resources needed to pursue successful grant acquisition strategies. By investing in their capacity, these grants would enable more people to secure funding and make a positive impact in their communities.

🔍 Word Search

Join us in celebrating the remarkable journey of Marilyn Crawford, a dedicated PTA member with a dream to secure funding for her school. When she discovered Mr. Grant Money's Grant Acquisition Success Guide, priced at $4,997, she embarked on a journey of learning, inspiration, and determination.

In this puzzle, discover the words related to the extraordinary adventures of Mr. Grant Money. Can you find all the hidden words that capture the essence of this remarkable story?

Now, here are the 14 words for the word search puzzle based on the story:

P	C	C	R	R	R	R	S	P	E	H	A	E	O
N	O	O	R	O	S	N	T	E	G	L	E	S	L
P	M	A	I	P	I	O	O	R	L	I	A	I	P
A	M	M	Y	A	T	I	R	S	C	N	C	L	E
I	U	A	M	R	A	S	Y	E	R	S	Q	O	D
D	N	R	P	T	A	I	T	V	A	P	U	O	I
H	I	I	I	N	Q	V	E	E	W	I	I	H	U
C	T	L	S	E	G	Y	L	R	F	R	S	C	G
R	Y	Y	D	R	R	F	L	A	O	A	I	S	V
A	S	N	O	S	A	U	I	N	R	T	T	Y	T
E	H	N	M	H	N	N	C	D	I	I	C	R	
S	E	I	N	I	T	D	G	E	E	O	O	I	T
E	F	S	H	P	T	S	D	I	L	N	N	U	O
R	C	U	S	S	C	R	A	T	P	I	N	T	S

Word list:

- INSPIRATION
- PTA
- GUIDE
- ACQUISITION
- GRANT
- PARTNERSHIPS
- COMMUNITY
- SCHOOL
- CRAWFORD
- STORYTELLING
- VISION
- FUNDS
- PERSEVERANCE
- RESEARCH
- MARILYN

"Marilyn's journey, driven by a limited budget and a determined spirit, demonstrates that with the right guidance, strategic insights, and the support of a passionate team, remarkable success in grant acquisition is achievable. Her story is a testament to the transformative power of vision and perseverance, regardless of financial constraints."

The Amazing Adventures of
MR GRANT MONEY

From Caribbean Waves to Grant Wins: Mr. Grant Money's Journey

Grant Acquisition Secrets Discovered Amidst Crystal Waters and Style

Mr. Grant Money, never one to shy away from elegance and style, found himself aboard a luxurious cruise ship bound for the beautiful shores of Jamaica. He had set aside three weeks for relaxation and reading, a rare chance to recharge and gather new insights that would benefit his clients in the world of grant acquisition.

As the ship glided through the crystal-clear waters of the Caribbean, Mr. Grant Money was stylishly overdressed, as always. His attire, by most people's standards, seemed excessive, but for Mr. Grant Money, it was a reflection of his unique personality. He was seated on the deck, in the exclusive VIP Captain's Quarters, reserved for a select few passengers who appreciated the finer things in life.

With a notebook and pen in hand, Mr. Grant Money began to read. It was not uncommon for him to devour three to four books in a week, for he knew that each page held the potential for new insights that could be skillfully applied to help his clients secure more grants.

On this particular day, he had picked up "The Law of Success" by Napoleon Hill, a timeless classic known for its wisdom on achieving success in various aspects of life. As he delved into the book, he couldn't help but think out loud about three intriguing points that he believed could be applied to a grant acquisition plan for the City of Dallas and their Housing Department:

1. Definite Chief Aim: Mr. Grant Money pondered the concept of a "definite chief aim," which Hill emphasized as a crucial step toward success. He realized that just as individuals needed a clear and specific goal to achieve success, grant acquisition plans required a well-defined purpose and mission. For the City of Dallas, this meant identifying the exact funding needs and how they would benefit the community.

2. Mastermind Alliance: Hill stressed the importance of forming a "mastermind alliance" with like-minded individuals who could provide support and expertise. Mr. Grant Money saw the potential for creating a network of experts and stakeholders in the grant acquisition process. By bringing together key players, the Housing Department could strengthen their proposals and increase their chances of winning grants.

3. Applied Faith: Hill's concept of "applied faith" resonated with Mr. Grant Money. He realized that in the world of grant acquisition, belief in the mission and the ability to execute the plan were essential. The City of Dallas needed to have unwavering faith in their vision for housing development, and they had to apply that belief with concrete action.

With these insights in mind, Mr. Grant Money closed the book and smiled, donning his stylish shades as he gazed into the warm Caribbean sun. He whispered to himself, "We're getting ready to score another touchdown for Big D! "Curiosity abounded among fellow passengers and the ship's crew. They all wanted to know who this elegant and distinguished figure was, and why he seemed to exude an air of wisdom and confidence. It wasn't long before the Captain and the waiters revealed his identity to the intrigued admirers.

"That," the Captain said with a knowing nod, **"is Mr. Grant Money.** He's a Master Grant Acquisition Specialist—**a man who works magic in getting grants."**

As the cruise ship continued its journey, Mr. Grant Money reveled in the thought of the opportunities ahead. He knew that the insights he had gathered would play a vital role in helping the City of Dallas secure the funding they needed to improve housing and make a positive impact on their community. His adventures in grant acquisition were far from over, and he was eager to bring his unique style and expertise to every challenge that lay ahead.

Exercise: "The Grant Acquisition Mastermind Alliance"

Mr. Grant Money's revelation about the importance of forming a "mastermind alliance" from his reading of Napoleon Hill's book can be a valuable approach in grant acquisition. This exercise encourages individuals or teams to create a mastermind alliance to enhance their grant-seeking strategies.

Objective: To establish a grant acquisition mastermind alliance that brings together individuals with diverse skills and expertise to strengthen grant applications and increase the chances of success.

Steps:

1. Identify Your Grant Acquisition Goals:
- Define your specific grant acquisition goals, whether you are an individual or part of an organization. What funding do you need, and for what purpose? Write down your goals.

2. Recruit Mastermind Partners:
- Identify individuals or colleagues who share an interest in securing grants and have complementary skills, expertise, or resources that can contribute to your grant-seeking efforts. Look for diversity in experience and knowledge.

3. Conduct a Mastermind Alliance Meeting:
- Organize an initial meeting or gathering with your chosen mastermind partners. Share your grant acquisition goals and explain the purpose of the alliance.

4. Define Roles and Expectations:
- Discuss and define the roles and responsibilities of each member within the mastermind alliance. Clarify expectations, including how often you will meet and what contributions are expected from each member.

5. Create a Shared Vision Statement:
- Collaboratively craft a vision statement that represents the goals and aspirations of your grant acquisition efforts. This statement should reflect the impact you aim to make in your community or organization.

6. Research and Expertise Sharing:

- Encourage members to share their knowledge and expertise related to grant acquisition. Each member should contribute insights, strategies, and research resources to strengthen your grant proposals.

7. Critique and Review Grant Proposals:

- Use the mastermind alliance to review and critique grant proposals. Members can provide constructive feedback to improve the quality and effectiveness of the applications.

8. Leverage Networking Opportunities:

- Exploit the collective network of the mastermind alliance to access new opportunities and contacts in the grant acquisition field. Attend events, webinars, or conferences together to expand your network.

9. Set Milestones and Deadlines:

- Establish milestones and deadlines for your grant acquisition plan. Break down your plan into manageable steps, and use the mastermind alliance to hold each other accountable for progress.

10. Applied Faith and Positive Mindset:

- Cultivate a mindset of "applied faith" within the mastermind alliance. Encourage and support each other in believing in the vision and taking action with confidence.

11. Regular Mastermind Meetings:

- Schedule regular meetings or check-ins with your alliance to discuss progress, challenges, and any adjustments to your grant acquisition strategy.

12. Celebrate Achievements:

- Celebrate your achievements as a team when you secure grant funding. Recognize the collective effort that contributed to your success.

By creating a grant acquisition mastermind alliance, you can tap into the collective wisdom, resources, and support of like-minded individuals, just as Mr. Grant Money's style and expertise made him a valuable asset in the grant acquisition world. Together, you can enhance your grant-seeking strategies and increase your chances of securing the funding needed to make a positive impact on your community or organization.

Discussion Questions

1. Mr. Grant Money reflects on three principles from Napoleon Hill's "The Law of Success" and considers their application to a grant acquisition plan for the City of Dallas. How might the concepts of "definite chief aim," "mastermind alliance," and "applied faith" be integrated into a successful grant acquisition strategy for a municipal department or nonprofit organization, and what specific actions could be taken to realize these principles?

2. The story mentions Mr. Grant Money's unique style and elegance. How important is personal branding and presentation for grant acquisition specialists, and what role does it play in establishing credibility and trust with potential funders and partners? Can an individual's personal style impact their success in the field of grant acquisition?

3. The story suggests that Mr. Grant Money's expertise could contribute to the City of Dallas securing funding for housing development. What are the key challenges and considerations involved in securing grants for housing and community development initiatives, and how can these insights be applied to real-world situations to enhance the chances of success?

4. Mr. Grant Money is described as a Master Grant Acquisition Specialist. What qualities, skills, and expertise do you think are essential for individuals in this role, and how can aspiring grant acquisition specialists develop these attributes to make a meaningful impact in the field of grant acquisition?

5. The story alludes to Mr. Grant Money's commitment to helping the City of Dallas and his anticipation of "scoring another touchdown." What is the significance of sports metaphors and analogies in the context of grant acquisition and achieving success? How might such language influence motivation and goal-setting in grant-seeking efforts?

💡 Big Idea "Grant Acquisition Cruise Retreat"

Inspired by Mr. Grant Money's Caribbean cruise experience, the concept of a "Grant Acquisition Cruise Retreat" could be developed. This retreat would offer a unique and luxurious opportunity for grant seekers, nonprofit leaders, and government officials to embark on a cruise focused on grant acquisition. Passengers would learn from grant experts, including Mr. Grant Money himself, as they sail to exotic destinations. Workshops, seminars, and one-on-one consultations would be conducted on board, teaching participants the art of securing grants while enjoying the elegance and style of a luxury cruise. The "Grant Acquisition Cruise Retreat" would provide a unique blend of education, relaxation, and networking, creating a memorable and productive experience for attendees.

🔍 Word Search

Join us on a luxurious Caribbean cruise with Mr. Grant Money, the man of style and substance, as he takes a rare break from the world of grant acquisition. On this three-week adventure, he delves into Napoleon Hill's 'The Law of Success,' searching for insights to benefit his clients. As he lounges in elegance, he contemplates three key principles: 'Definite Chief Aim,' 'Mastermind Alliance,' and 'Applied Faith,' and their potential for the City of Dallas's grant acquisition.

In this puzzle, discover the words related to the extraordinary adventures of Mr. Grant Money. Can you find all the hidden words that capture the essence of this remarkable story?

Now, here are the 15 words for the word search puzzle based on the story:

S	S	A	A	D	A	L	L	A	S	I	E	E	E
I	S	B	C	J	A	M	E	S	E	T	N	S	O
L	U	E	A	A	C	B	A	S	N	S	Q	M	T
R	C	E	R	M	Q	N	O	A	T	C	A	M	S
B	C	I	I	A	U	N	R	S	S	A	N	I	
L	E	E	B	I	I	G	M	G	T	C	A	B	N
R	S	C	B	C	S	C	H	E	S	U	R	R	S
S	S	N	E	A	I	M	R	O	T	A	C	E	I
T	I	A	A	U	T	M	A	U	U	I	U	A	G
Y	B	G	N	O	I	T	E	T	M	S	N	D	H
L	I	E	L	N	O	N	A	N	T	D	I	I	T
E	O	L	D	Y	N	S	V	I	S	I	O	N	S
G	A	E	C	O	M	M	U	N	I	T	Y	G	G
A	R	E	L	A	X	A	T	I	O	N	S	A	A

CARIBBEAN
GRANT
SUCCESS
DALLAS
COMMUNITY
INSIGHTS
ACQUISITION
HOUSING
MASTERMIND
JAMAICA
RELAXATION
ELEGANCE
STYLE
READING
VISION

"The enigmatic gentleman on the cruise, known as Mr. Grant Money, exemplified the power of wisdom and style. His insights from 'The Law of Success' offered a fresh perspective on grant acquisition, showing how clear purpose, collaboration, and unwavering belief can pave the way for success. His aura of elegance and knowledge left a lasting impression on all who encountered him."

AFTERWARD

As you reach the final pages of The Amazing Adventures of Mr. Grant Money, Volume 1, I hope you've been both entertained and enlightened by the captivating stories of our enigmatic protagonist, Mr. Grant Money. Through his remarkable adventures, you've explored the world of grants and philanthropy in an entirely new light.

These stories are not just tales of daring exploits and awe-inspiring achievements. They are also valuable lessons in grant acquisition, each with its unique insights and wisdom. However, the true magic happens when you put these lessons into practice. Remember, knowledge without action is like a locked treasure chest; it holds immense potential, but only when you open it does its true value become apparent.

It's important to recognize that in the world of grant acquisition, we all start at ground zero. What separates the triumphant from the rest is the determination to progress beyond that initial point. After reading these stories, take a moment to reflect on the lessons they impart and how you can apply them to your own journey in grant acquisition.

And there's no need to stop here! Mr. Grant Money's adventures continue with even more fascinating tales in Volumes 2 through 5. As you embark on these new journeys, embrace the valuable insights they offer. Keep in mind that knowledge, like a never-ending treasure trove, continues to expand. By continuing to learn and adapt, you too can achieve remarkable results in the world of grants and philanthropy.

If you're looking for further guidance and resources, consider visiting GrantCentralUSA.com and GrantAcquisition.com. These platforms offer a wealth of tools, courses, and expert advice to enhance your grant acquisition skills.

Remember, the key to success in grant acquisition is not just in learning but in applying what you've learned. As Mr. Grant Money has demonstrated, each adventure is an opportunity for growth, and your journey is no different. The power to make a difference in your community and beyond is within your grasp.

So, gear up for the next volumes of Mr. Grant Money's incredible adventures, and keep striving to transform your grant acquisition endeavors into triumphant tales of your own. Your journey is just beginning, and there's no limit to what you can achieve. The world of grants and philanthropy is waiting for your story to unfold, and the possibilities are limitless.

ABOUT THE AUTHOR

Rodney Walker is a man on a mission. He's dedicated his life to helping others secure funding for their projects and dreams. As the President of Grant Central USA, a grant development training firm internationally known for helping organizations land six-figure and seven-figure grants and shave months off the time it takes to get funded, Rodney has helped clients raise over half a billion dollars in grants!

He's also an author of numerous books, online courses and the founder of two popular grant writing conferences: The Education Grants Conference and First Responders Grants Conference. Grant Central USA has also partnered with several universities, including Regis University, Hawaii University, Oklahoma University, National University, Cal Poly University, and Florida Atlantic University.

Rodney is even the host of four podcasts: Get Funded with Rodney, Grant Writing Today, Grant Business Show, and Schools Winning Grants. He oversees Grant Success Advisors, an elite network of approved licensees who deliver today's leading training in grant development systems.

He has an extensive network of high-level contacts, including his Grant Writers Association group on Linkedin with over 15,000+ members.

Considered a national authority in the grant industry, Grant Central USA's clients have included, The Magic Johnson Foundation, the George W. Bush Foundation, Ben Guillory and Danny Glover of the Robey Theatre Company, Hawaii State Teachers Association, United Way, Habitat for Humanity, and numerous school districts and city governments.

Rodney has produced over 730 videos on grant development on his popular YouTube channel and has taught over 240,000 people how to improve their grant writing efforts. "We have been helping our clients successfully get funded and launch new careers in grant writing since 2006 across the U.S. and worldwide, giving them both the competence and the confidence to win the grants at a high level."

He says his primary specialty is "Getting our clients funded with six-figure and seven-figure grants while helping grant professionals get paid what they are worth!"

In addition to his leadership experience at Grant Central USA, he has years of experience in Business and Professional Development in various sectors. He has been a sought-after expert in grant professional development, coaching, and the law of success.

As a media personality, he has interviewed numerous celebrities, including Snoop Dogg, Heisman Trophy Winners: Reggie Bush, Charles Woodson, Professional Boxer Laila Ali, America's Next Top Model Season 19 Winner: Laura James, NBA Champions: Draymond Green, Matt Barnes, National College Football Champions: Coach Mack Brown, and Vince Young, and countless others.

It's safe to say that Rodney knows his stuff regarding grants and working with champions!

GRANT MONEY MAGNET™

I am the Grant Money Magnet™, a relentless force that navigates the intricate maze of grant acquisition with unwavering determination and a strategic mind. Challenges are not obstacles; they are opportunities waiting to be seized. With every hurdle, I rise, armed with innovative solutions, pushing the boundaries of what's possible. My curiosity is my compass, guiding me through the maze of grant landscapes, uncovering hidden opportunities and transforming challenges into triumphs.

In the realm of grant development campaigns, I am the orchestrator of a symphony that goes beyond the basics of mere grant writing. My daily actions are a testament to my commitment, with well-defined grant goals propelling me forward. I am not a lone warrior; I am part of a powerful grant team, where collaboration amplifies our impact. Together, we transcend the ordinary, transforming aspirations into tangible results.

Grant funding doesn't elude me; I attract it with an irresistible magnetic force. My mind is a powerhouse of ideas, a generator of solutions that resonate with the aspirations of benefactors and the needs of society. Relentlessness is my mantra; there's no door I can't open, no avenue left unexplored. I don't just pursue grants; I nurture relationships, cultivating a network of allies who share my passion for impact. In my grant pursuit, I don't just raise funds; I raise friends and partners, forging alliances that extend beyond transactions into enduring collaborations.

As the architect of my grant destiny, I recognize that true power lies not just in acquiring funds but in the collective strength of a united effort. I am not merely a seeker of grants; I am a catalyst for transformative change. With each campaign, I etch my mark on the maze of philanthropy, weaving a narrative of impact that transcends the ordinary. Together with my grant team, I shape a future where challenges bow before innovation, and the resonance of our collaborative endeavors echoes through the corridors of progress. Grant by grant, we sculpt a legacy that stands as a testament to the limitless potential of unified action and unwavering dedication.

Recite and embrace the power of this statement daily; let its resonance shape your mindset and fuel your unwavering commitment to grant success.

GRANTOPOLY ROYAL RULES

Dive into a realm of funding mastery with Mr. Grant Money's 10 Grantopoly Royal Rules For Engagement - your strategic guide to securing maximum funding for your organization. Revisit these rules often and witness your grant success soar as you put them into practice! 🚀💲 #GrantMastery #FundingSuccess

1. 🎯 **Master the Mission:** Clearly articulate your organization's mission in every proposal, demonstrating an unwavering commitment to your cause.

2. 🌟 **Impact is King:** Highlight the tangible, life-changing impact of your projects; grantors want to see real results.

3. 🤝 **Build Strategic Alliances:** Showcase partnerships with other organizations to demonstrate a united front in achieving common goals.

4. 📊 **Data Speaks Louder:** Back your proposals with compelling data and statistics that underscore the urgency and necessity of your work.

5. 📖 **Storytelling Magic:** Craft narratives that evoke empathy, connecting the funder emotionally to your mission and beneficiaries.

6. 💰 **Budget Brilliance:** Develop meticulously detailed budgets that align with project goals and ensure every dollar is well-spent.

7. 📈 **Transparent Metrics:** Articulate clear and measurable outcomes, outlining how the funding will drive positive change.

8. 🌐 **Engage the Community:** Illustrate strong community involvement and support, reflecting a broad network invested in your success.

9. 🔄 **Continuous Learning:** Demonstrate a commitment to improvement through feedback loops and adaptive strategies.

10. 🙏 **Express Gratitude:** Always express sincere gratitude for the grantor's consideration, building a foundation for long-term partnerships.

MR. GRANT MONEY'S IDIOMS

Welcome to a world of financial creativity and linguistic flair! In this collection, you'll find ten unique "Mr. Grant Money" idioms crafted to add a touch of wit and imagination to your discussions about grants and funding opportunities. These idioms are not just expressions; they're windows into the dynamic and often challenging realm of grant acquisition. Enjoy more of these with new ones in the next volumes.

1. **Counting Mr. Grant's blessings:**
Meaning: Refers to someone who is fortunate or financially well-off due to receiving a grant or unexpected financial assistance.

2. **Chasing the Grant Dragon:**
Meaning: Engaging in relentless pursuit of financial opportunities, especially grants, with uncertain outcomes.

3. **Granting Wishes on a Shoestring:**
Meaning: Achieving desired outcomes with limited financial resources, often through strategic grant utilization.

4. **The Grant Rainmaker:**
Meaning: A person or entity that consistently attracts grants and financial support, seemingly effortlessly.

5. **Counting Grant Sheep:**
Meaning: Having difficulty falling asleep due to financial worries, especially related to grant funding and resources.

6. **Dancing for Grant Gold:**
Meaning: Putting in extraordinary effort or going to great lengths to secure grant funding.

7. **Granting the Goose that Lays Golden Eggs:**
Meaning: Successfully managing and preserving a valuable source of ongoing grant income.

8. **Caught in the Grant Web:**
Meaning: Facing complexities and challenges associated with managing multiple grant-funded projects.

9. **The Grant Magician:**
Meaning: An individual with exceptional skills in obtaining and managing grants, making the process seem magical.

10. **Granting a Mountain out of a Molehill:**
Meaning: Exaggerating the impact or significance of a grant, especially during discussions or presentations.

INFORMATIONAL INTERVIEW

Informational interviews are an excellent way to gain valuable insights and knowledge from experienced grant professionals and grant makers. By engaging in conversations with experts in the field, you can enhance your understanding, learn best practices, and foster your continuous growth and development in the world of grant funding.

Instructions:

1. **Identify Potential Interviewees:**
   - Create a list of grant professionals, grant makers, and other individuals with relevant insights whom you would like to interview. Consider factors such as expertise, experience, and industry focus.

2. **Reach Out:**
   - Craft a polite and concise email introducing yourself and explaining your interest in an informational interview. Request a convenient time for a meeting, either in person, over the phone, or via video call.

3. **Prepare Questions:**
   - Develop a list of thoughtful questions to guide your conversation. Tailor these questions to the individual's expertise and experiences. Be sure to ask about challenges they've faced, successes they've had, and advice they can offer.

4. **Schedule the Interview:**
   - Once you receive a positive response, schedule a time for the informational interview. Be respectful of their time and come prepared with your questions.

5. **Conduct the Interview:**
   - During the interview, actively listen, take notes, and ask follow-up questions. Be respectful of their time constraints and focus on extracting valuable insights.

6. **Reflect and Analyze:**
   - After each interview, take some time to reflect on the key takeaways. Consider how the information can be applied to your own work and goals.

7. **Thank You Note:**
   - Send a thank-you email expressing your gratitude for their time and insights. Mention specific points from the interview that were particularly helpful.

INFORMATIONAL INTERVIEW

Interviewee Information:

Name:
Title:
Organization:
Contact Information:
Date of Interview:

Interview Questions:

1. What led you to pursue a career in grant writing /management/grant making?
2. Can you share a significant challenge you faced in your career and how you overcame it?
3. What are the key skills and qualities you believe are crucial for success in this field?
4. How do you stay updated on the latest trends and changes in the grant industry?
5. Can you provide insights into your most successful grant project? What made it successful?
6. What advice do you have for someone looking to advance their career in grant management/grant making?
7. Are there any common misconceptions about working in grant-related roles that you'd like to address?

Key Takeaways:

Learnings:
Actionable Steps:
Connections Made:

Next Steps:

Identify Additional Contacts:
Schedule Next Informational Interview:
Implement Insights into Your Work:

This worksheet is designed to guide you through the process of conducting informational interviews and extracting valuable information to support your continuous growth and development in the field of grant funding. Good luck!

Take Your Grant Game To The Next Level With These...

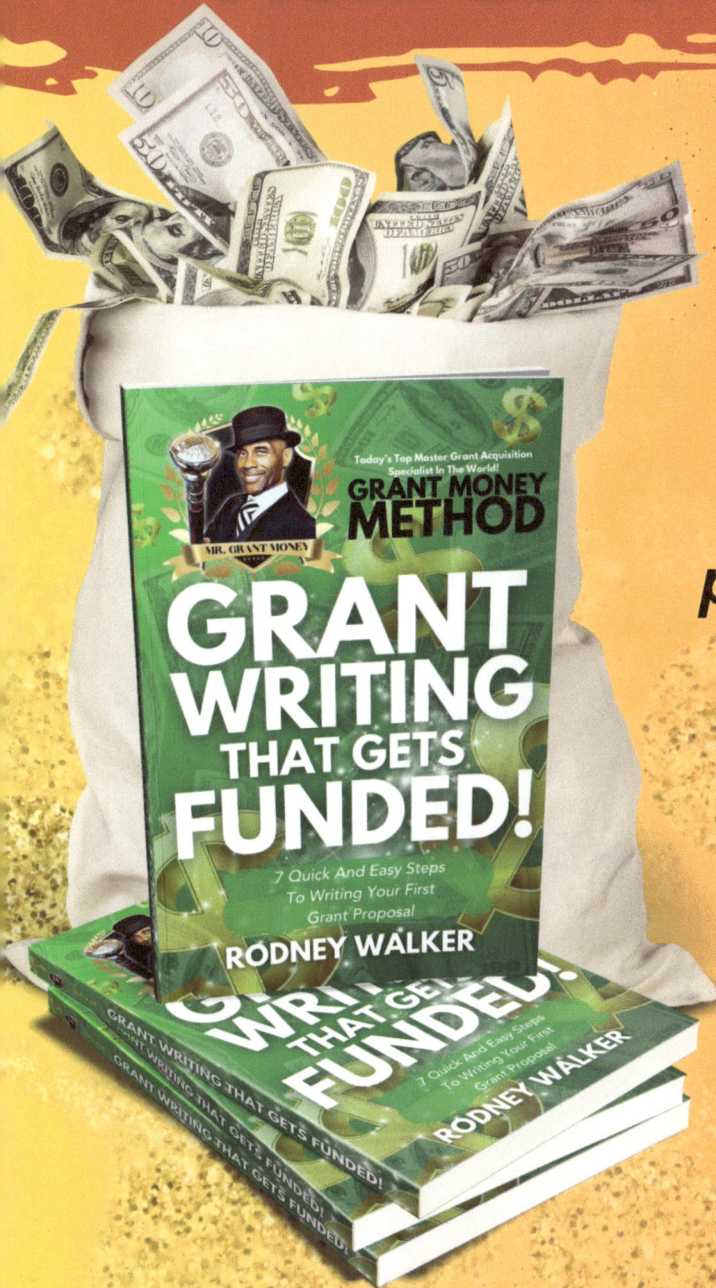

"Rodney is a grant genius! His courses are well thought out and clear, making the process of learning grant writing easier."
- Elena Esparza, Procurement/Contract Administrator

Transform your grant proposals into lucrative successes with my proven strategies that have raised millions.

"I hit my benchmark goal of $350,000.00!"
- Rebecca Laharia

"Thank you so much for your help. Probably not a day has gone by that I didn't use something."
- Evelyn Barker, Director of Grants and Special Project at University of Texas

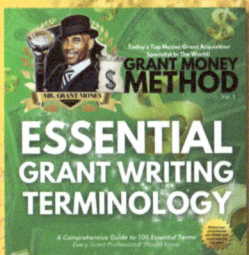

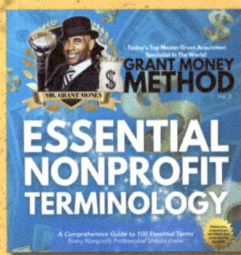

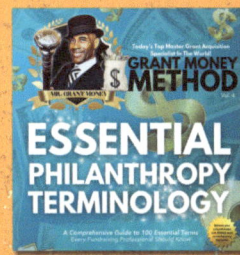

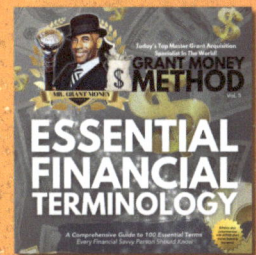

Boost your confidence in grant writing, fundraising, and finance! Elevate your communication skills with the **Fundraising Fundamentals Vocabulary Builder Series** – *100 essential terms in each series.* Invest in knowledge, empower your success!

MGM Music to Get You Going 🎷 and 🎶 Keep You Soaring!

Music has the power to make life and learning more joyful. Get ready to have a blast with Mr. Grant Money Music, where every tune is fun, upbeat, and filled with positivity. These story-driven songs not only entertain but also educate and inspire, making your journey both enjoyable and enriching. 🎶

MRGRANTMONEY
HAPPY NEW YEAR

Dive into a symphony of stories and inspiration with Mr. Grant Money Music, where every note is a step toward greater success.

You can enjoy Mr. Grant Money Music on most major streaming platforms, including Spotify, Apple Music, and Amazon Music, bringing inspiration and positivity right to your favorite device. 🎧

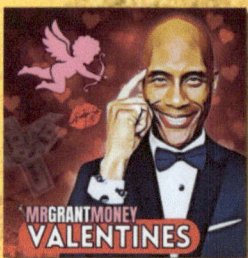

Diverse Musical Flavors to Satisfy Every Listening Craving

MRGRANTMONEY VALENTINES

Discover **MRGRANTMONEY**

MRGRANTMONEY HAPPY HALLOWEEN

thankfulness **MRGRANTMONEY**

JINGLE FEET

Topical and Seasonal Themes

Enjoy our themed musical sessions that align with the seasons and current events, offering fresh perspectives and innovative ideas from today's Top Master Grant Acquisition Specialist, Mr. Grant Money!

Experience Our Other Dynamic Series with Mr. Grant Money!

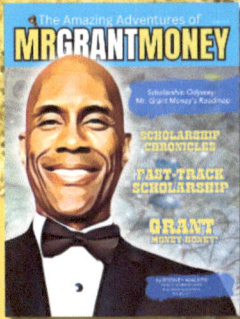

Scholarship Odyssey: Mr. Grant Money's Roadmap
Vol. 1
ISBN 979-8-89725-000-4

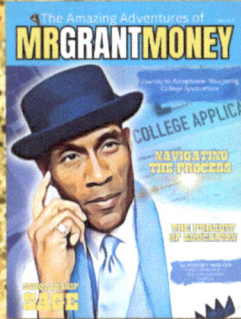

Journey To Acceptance: Navigating College Applications
Vol. 2
ISBN 979-8-89725-001-1

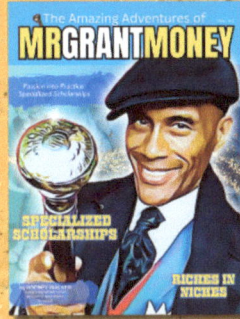

Passion Into Practice: Specialized Scholarship
Vol. 3
ISBN 979-8-89725-002-8

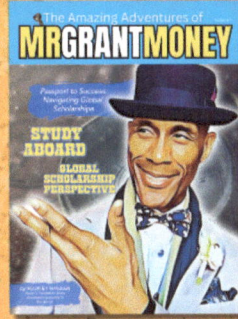

Passport To Success: Navigating Global Scholarships
Vol. 4
ISBN 979-8-89725-003-5

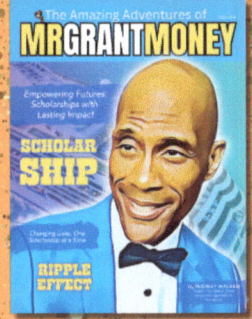

Empowering Futures: Scholarships With Lasting Impact
Vol. 5
ISBN 979-8-89725-004-2

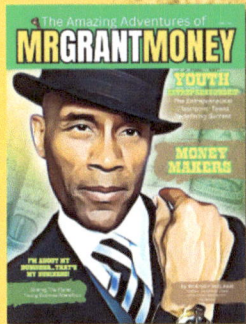

The Entrepreneurial Classroom: Teens Redefining Success
Vol. 1
ISBN 979-8-89725-005-9

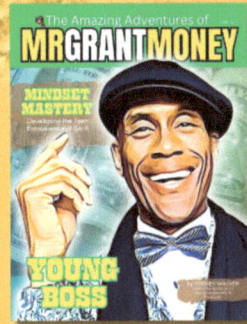

Mindset Mastery: Developing The Teen Entrepreneurial Spirit
Vol. 2
ISBN 979-8-89725-006-6

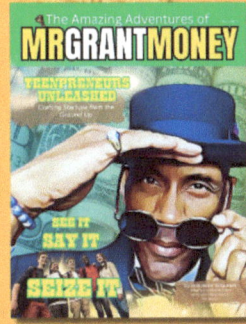

Teenpreneurs Unleashed: Crafting Startups From The Ground Up
Vol. 3
ISBN 979-8-89725-007-3

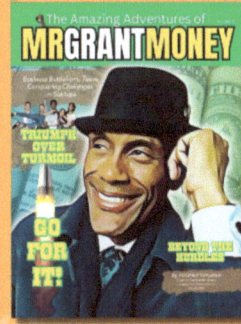

Business Battlefront: Teens Conquering Challenges In Startups
Vol. 4
ISBN 979-8-89725-008-0

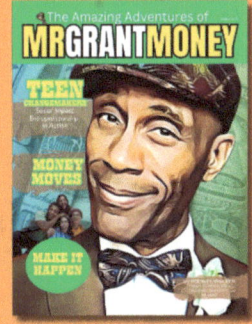

Teen Changemakers: Social Impact Entrepreneurship in Action
Vol. 5
ISBN 979-8-89725-009-7

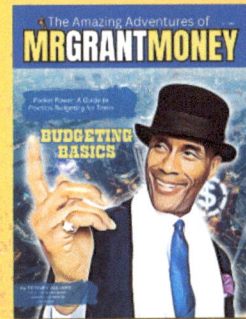

Pocket Power: A Guide to Practical Budgeting for Teens
Vol. 1
ISBN 979-8-89725-010-3

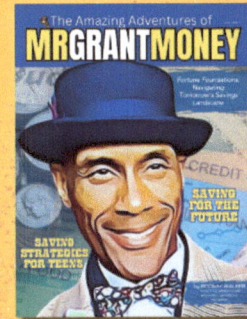

Fortune Foundations: Navigating Tomorrow's Savings Landscape
Vol. 2
ISBN 979-8-89725-011-0

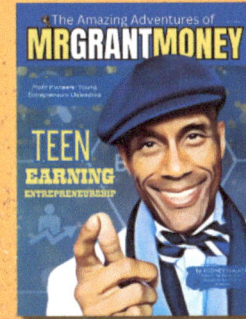

Profit Pioneers: Young Entrepreneurs Unleashed
Vol. 3
ISBN 979-8-89725-012-7

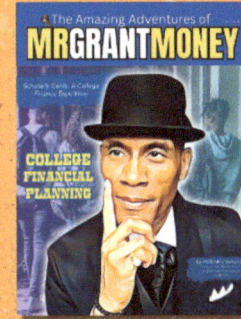

Scholarly Cents: A College Finance Expedition
Vol. 4
ISBN 979-8-89725-013-4

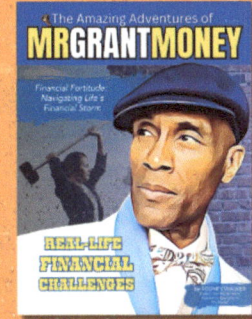

Financial Fortitude: Navigating Life's Financial Storm
Vol. 5
ISBN 979-8-89725-014-1

Enjoy More Amazing Adventures with Mr. Grant Money!

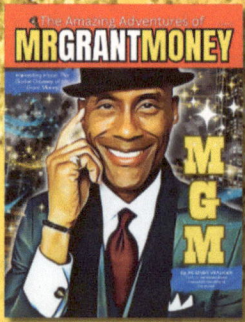

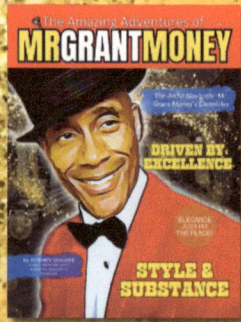

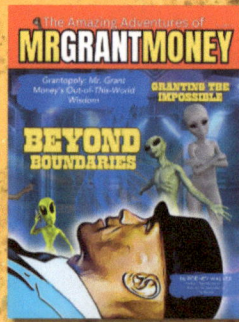

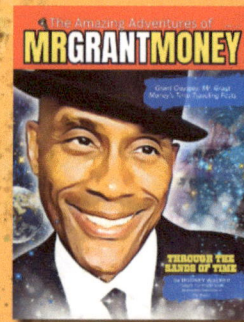

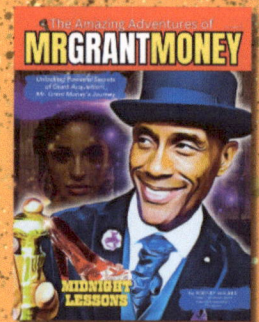

Gain Exclusive Access To Companion Resources & Bonus Materials at MrGrantMoney.com and GrantCentralUsa.com

LICENSED

Bring the transformative Adventures and lessons of Mr. Grant Money to your educational institution or organization by **acquiring your license today**. Enjoy exclusive access to a wealth of online resources, such as special reports, worksheets, videos, audio training, discounts, and more, elevating the entire experience to the next level!

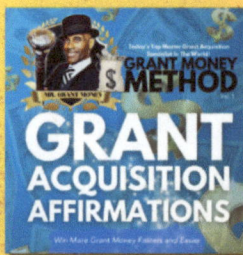

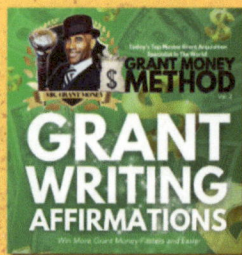

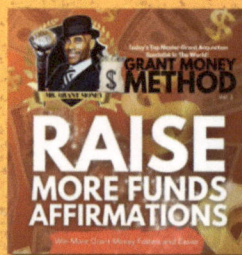

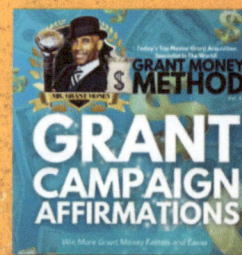

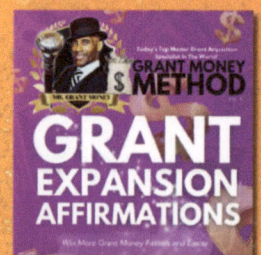

Envision and affirm your grant success in the same proactive spirit as Mr. Grant Money. **Experience the power of these daily affirmations** to inspire and motivate your journey toward success!

www.ingramcontent.com/pod-product-compliance
Lightning Source LLC
Chambersburg PA
CBHW041449210326
41599CB00004B/193